This book is dedicated to Archangel Gabriel; God's
messenger angel, the angel of communication

About the Shrew Sisters:

While Diane does the actual writing, Terryee is the one with all the scoop. She's got that psychic thing going on with the angels. Diane's insanely jealous of it, but she tries to hide it well. Oh yeah, and Terryee's name rhymes with Marie. It's Marie with a T. It drives us crazy when people say "Terry" or "Terry-yee." And Diane's last name rhymes with Gucci. "Boo-chee." We hate it when we're mispronounced.

Terryee Abbott

Terryee has been clairvoyant since she can remember. She's built a successful enterprise with her brand AngelCoaches, helping countless people through divine guidance and common sense. Terryee is a psychic, spiritual counselor, light healer, and radio host. She's been an advisor to celebrities, politicians, and CEO's of major corporations. Contact her at AngelCoaches.org or find the AngelCoaches community page on Facebook.

Diane Bucci

Diane is an author, motivational speaker, and private spiritual coach. Diane won the Irwin Award for 'Most Inspirational Book 2012' for **The Return of Mikey**, which detailed her autistic son's life, death, and life after death phenomenon. She recently published, **Facebook: The Greatest Passive Aggressive Weapon EVER.** Contact: Diane@DianeBucci.com or on Facebook at "DianeBucci.com" and "The Return of Mikey" pages. On Twitter @ReturnOfMikey.

Table of Contents

"You mean there's a LAW that says he has to be ATTRACTED to me?"

A psychic and a humorist explain metaphysics in terms you can understand...and actually use to improve your life

Terryee and I had a vision of creating a book that would put "The Law of Attraction" in layman's terms, and explain what all the hoopla is about to the non-metaphysical crowd, who we refer to as "normal people." We consider ourselves a part of this crowd, although our platforms might not suggest it. By platforms, we don't mean shoes with risers, although Terryee is fond of the higher elevation they lend her. By higher elevation, we don't mean higher consciousness; we mean she's short.

Terryee is a psychic, and I am a bereaved mother who believes her dead son's spirit is still alive and well and up to his usual pranks. I authored a book, **The Return of Mikey**, which gives an accounting of my experiences after Mikey's death. Terryee talks to dead people. I talk to groups of live people who have dead people in their lives. I call them Grief Support Groups.

But aside from our unconventional spiritual beliefs, we are both quite normal and successful. We've made remarkable achievements in our careers, our personal lives are fulfilling, and we both have that "inner peace" thing going for us.

Did we accomplish our achievements by using some strange immutable scientific "law" that is a big secret to everyone but the metaphysics? Do we have weird old dead people channeling their ancient wisdom into our thoughts during meditation? When I am laying on the couch vegging out, can I really call that "meditation?" Well, I do, but only if a "new age" person calls during my "meditation." If a normal person's calling, I just say I'm cleaning the house – or some other lie that will make me sound like I'm not just being lazy.

No, I'm not knocking meditation. I wish I could experience that out-of-body consciousness that serious meditators say they achieve. I also wish I could hear angels and guides talking to me when I'm in the waking state. I wouldn't have so many speeding tickets.

But unlike most "normal people," I don't discount the claims of others who say they have these abilities. Au contraire, I've witnessed the validity of their outlandish predictions in my own life, and therefore am a believer. I've applied the wisdom of these "predictors" in my personal and professional pursuits, with great success.

So while Terryee and I are not professing to know about any secret laws of the universe, we both know how to get what we want: Men, money, professional accolades, personal satisfaction and peace. And we use a form of focused thought that some would call positive thinking, others would call the Law of Attraction, but we just call it believing in our dreams. Not the nightmarish kind of dreams where you're falling off of something, mind you. *Day*dreams. Fantasizing about the kind of life we want, and believing our fantasies are going to come true. Is that living in la-la land? Perhaps, but it's worked for us and many others. So call it whatever you want, but don't call it "new age" garbage. It's an old age philosophy that has seen resurgence in recent years under various guises.

We're going to teach you *constructive* daydreaming through manifesting techniques. The word *daydreaming* connotes wasting time, but manifesting is time well spent. It's money in the bank, and the love of your life to help spend it. It's the difference between fantasizing about a better tomorrow, and making it come to fruition. Focused intent on believing your dreams will manifest into reality is a practiced thought process. Failures and setbacks along the way make the practicing difficult, at times, but not impossible.

So what better reason do you need to read this book than to have two successful women tell you that daydreaming is highly productive, financially profitable, and emotionally fulfilling? We thought so. Not only that, but we *believe* so. Thinking and Believing are two different concepts, and we are going to teach you how to do the latter, even when others tell you you're a crazy dreamer. By changing your thoughts, you will learn to believe in your own ability to succeed and get what you want. Sounds easy, but it's not. Thought patterns are deeply ingrained in our psyche. But the fact is we can change our negative thinking patterns to draw positive situations into our lives. While this idea has been echoed over and over in different terminology in varying philosophical jargon, the same basic principle is underlying all that positive thinking/like attracting/secretly powerful mumbo-jumbo. And since it's worked for so many others, isn't it worth a try?

You have nothing to lose but a little time fantasizing, which you would do anyway. This book is going to help you turn that idle "wasted" time spent dreaming of a better life, into a prosperous time of manifesting those dreams. You've got the dreams already inside you. Add a little dose of focused intention, and you're on your way to making them a reality.

Over the years, Terryee has heard every type of story imaginable from her clients who enlist her psychic services for personal readings. Naturally gifted with clairvoyance, she's gained further enlightenment through working with so many people who have many different kinds of problems, but the same underlying motivations. We're sharing many of their stories with you to illustrate human behavior, although we have changed the names to protect the idiots – or, make that – the innocent.

What is the Law of Attraction, and When was this Law Enacted?

Although the theory of a universal law of 'like attracting like' has been around since William Walker Atkinson used the phrase in 1906, in recent years it's gotten a lot of attention. Think back to the earlier revolution of the power of positive thinking. Now add a decade of techno-psychology research. The Law of Attraction takes positive thinking one step farther. It turns *thinking* into *believing*, and *goal-setting* into *manifesting*. We're going to explain how to use the principles of this mysterious law of attraction in your own life, and also take a look at some of the common roadblocks where people tend to get stuck. But we won't call it a law, because you might be tempted to break it, and then we would have to call the metaphysical police on you.

> "You mean there's a law that says he has to be attracted to me?" a caller asked. Terryee began trying to explain the law of attraction to the woman who called for a psychic reading regarding a relationship. The caller wanted a romantic relationship to develop with a man she worked with. By the woman's account, this man was a selfless saint dressed up as a Greek God. He reportedly spent a lot of time maintaining his physical appearances, while the woman admittedly wore twenty extra pounds from her love of fast food. The man devoted countless hours to charity work, while

the woman spent her evenings watching reality television.

"You need to *be* the partner you desire for yourself," Terryee explained. "If you want a man who is physically fit, you need to be physically fit yourself. If you want to spend three hours a night watching bad acting, then you will attract a man who does the same. Do you understand the law of attraction?"

"Sure," the woman replied. "So, is he attracted to me or what?"

Everyone wants to call a psychic and hear the answers that will make them happy. Terryee has built her reputation on her honesty as much as her ability to commune with the spirit world. I am a life-long believer in positivity myself, and I've achieved greater success after becoming a protégé of Terryee's successful coaching.

For sake of giving credit to the originators of this theory, and also to prove that we've done our homework, here's a little history on 'the Law of Attraction.' In 1906, Atkinson stated in his book, **Thought Vibration or the Law of Attraction in the Thought World**, "like attracts like." The writings of William Quan Judge and Annie Besant both contained the phrase "law of attraction" in 1915 and 1919 respectively. Besant thought it represented a form of karma, and she compared it to gravitation. Israel Regardie published books based on what he termed "a universal law of attraction," and his 1937 offering, **The Art of True Healing, A Treatise on the Mechanism of Prayer and the Operation of the Law of Attraction in Nature** was a self-help book. His book taught focused meditation to help the mind learn how to heal itself on both physical and spiritual levels.

So why did it take a hundred years for this ideology to start catching on? We can thank Esther and Jerry Hicks for their 2006 book, **The Law of Attraction: The Basics of the Teachings of Abraham.** This best-selling book has many people following the Hicks' guide to making this universal "law" work to their advantage.

But there were others who preceded them with the same ideology, only different terminology. Everyone has a different slant on the power of thought. We don't care what you call it. We only care that it works. Terryee feels comfortable talking about the Law of Attraction, while I feel more comfortable talking about the power of positive thought. But we both agree that we are essentially doing the same basic thing: believing our fantasies will come true. For some reason, that doesn't sound as intelligent as Laws and Powers do. Laws and Powers sound much more impressive when people ask us to share our secrets for success. You never hear someone like Bill Gates saying he believes his fantasies are going to come true. He might sound like a pervert. But if you adhere to the advice in our book and someday find yourself being asked to share your secrets for success, we'll understand if you feel more comfortable saying, "Laws and Powers," as long as you give us the proverbial wink-wink when you say this.

The main point is, to achieve the abundance you desire in life, love, and money, you have to believe you are not only capable of achieving it, but you are worthy of having it. We've found most of the other books on manifesting abundance are leaving out that crucial part: feeling worthy. It's like reading a book that teaches you how to dance the tango when you haven't learned how to walk yet.

Counseling countless people through real life issues, including grief, we have discovered that many people are not successful with manifesting through positive thought because of one common roadblock: low self-worth. It's necessary to delve deeper into one's own psyche to understand what is inhibiting you from believing you are worthy and capable of achieving prosperity in love and life.

People come from one of two places. They either come from love or they come from fear. You can choose to act in love or *react* in fear. The principles of the positive thought philosophy demand you are coming from an abundant place of love. Unfortunately, many people are trapped in the hall of mirrors called Fear. Fear of being unworthy; Fear of being less-than; Fear of getting passed over for someone who is deemed more worthy; Fear of loss of love, loss of image, loss of security. All of these fears are hiding behind the fragile wall of the ego. While the ego is supposed to protect our self-worth, our fears erode that wall. As anyone over the age of 18 can tell you, the most arrogant, egotistical people are usually the most insecure. Outwardly big egos do not mean internally high self-esteem exists. It's usually a smoke and mirrors ruse.

The law of attraction essentially means you're relying on the invisible world of energy to help you attract what you want. Harnessing the positive energy that brings you towards your goals is easy when you're in a positive state of mind. The problem is.... how many of us are always in a good mood? Be honest here. How many times are you just frikkin pissed off? Or jealous as fuck? Your life is shit! (No, the angels don't care if we use foul language. Only *people* christen some words as "bad.")

So in order to ride that wave of positivity, you have to let go of all your *nega*tivity. Easier said than done. Terryee and I were getting tired of looking at new age higher consciousness books, and finding the authors tried to make it look all airy-fairy. Like you can just float on into your happy state of higher consciousness when you just got dumped, fired, or in a major fight with your mother. You get paid tomorrow, but your rent is due, and now you have to pick between paying the rent or fixing your car, which just got towed to the shop today. You're starving and you have no food in the house. The only restaurant within walking distance has dinner salads starting at $9.99 and up.

You only have $4.93 to your name. So you sit down with a cup of hot water and a tea bag that's been flying around in your pantry for a hundred years – probably has gnats in it - and you crack open a book that somebody gave you about angelic wisdom and the law of attraction. The picture on the cover looks pretty enough, so you begin reading passages written by the millionaire author, who is telling you to just close your eyes and you will begin communing with the angelic spirit world, and everything in your life will suddenly become hunky-dory. The hell it will. Your life sucks right now. And it's gonna suck for a while longer.

My favorite line from Terryee came after she felt guided to do something that led to a great deal of pain for her.

> "Those damn cloud-huggin' angels don't know how *hard* it is down here!" she cried. "Why did they tell me to do that?"

Personally, I felt secretly gratified to know a psychic with the ability to get first-hand advice from higher powers actually felt like she got the wrong signals from time to time. I know *I* have, and I didn't hear any angelic voices telling me to run that red light.

So we're going to try to put things in terminology that you can relate to, even if you don't agree with us. Maybe a snippet of it will make some sense, and you'll give it a try while you're drinking your gnat-infested tea.

Self-Worth Saboteurs

In finding one's own value, the focus should be placed on human character qualities. Are you kind? Compassionate? Sincere? Honest? Loving? Unselfish? Forgiving? Those are all qualities to value. They are worth something to you in the end. Those qualities enrich the lives of the people around you, and those are qualities God would smile on. God doesn't value your soul for the car that it's riding in. What qualities of value do you contribute to the lives of the people around you? No, your good looks don't count.

When you begin focusing on the love and happiness you want to attract in your own life, you first need to determine if you're a source of those things for others. Do you share your love openly, or do you selfishly dole out parcels of appreciation only when you gain something in return? You're defeating your own intentions for abundance if you are stuck in negative behavior patterns. We're listing a few of the top contenders here.

Selfishness

Most people who are selfish would never see themselves as such. Here are a few questions to ask yourself. If you answer 'yes' to any of them, then other people around you probably view you as a selfish person. That's right. You're not as sweet as you thought you were.

> Do you frequently feel you've been cheated out of something tangible?

> Do you feel others always get more?

> Do you secretly resent it when someone else gets something you want?

> Do you have a mental list of all the reasons why you should have been given something that another person got? Do you readily share that list with anyone who will listen to why the other person didn't deserve to get what you wanted?

> Do you immediately regret it when you share something that's tangible?

> Do you suffer from "Giver's Remorse" rather than "Buyer's Remorse?"

> Do you feel there is not enough to go around, and you can justify why you should get whatever there is?

If you struggle with selfishness, you are living in a constant state of feeling like you don't have enough. You're always looking around and wishing you had more, even if you have the most. You need to examine why you feel that way. It may be an issue from childhood or it could be a previous life experience that you came here to work through.

Selfishness is one of those feelings that constrict our energy. If you are attracting abundance, your energy should feel expansive. Selfishness constricts our energy as we focus inward instead of outward. Our attention is solely focused on feeding our ego's demand for visible objects that prove we are more deserving than others. The more we accumulate, the more our ego thinks it will be satisfied. But it never is.

Self-worth does not come from the hoarding of objects, money, or attention. And the more we display selfish behavior, the more our higher self looks down on us with disdain. The communication between your higher consciousness and your ego determines your own self-worth. If your heart knows you are loving and unselfish, your head will acknowledge that you are worthy of self-esteem. If your attention is solely focused on acquiring every piece of the pie, your higher self will not be so kind as to give you a clear conscience. Yep, your conscience has a conscience.

Jealousy

It's natural to feel jealous at times, and even healthy. If we didn't feel a tad bit envious of someone else's accomplishments, we wouldn't have much motivation to accomplish anything ourselves. It's natural to feel jealous when a romantic partner breaks up with you to date someone else. Your heart strings are still attached to that person, and you long to be the object of their affection. Those are normal forms of jealousy that everyone experiences.

But there are some people who are inherently jealous by nature, and their jealousy consumes much of their thinking. Once again, the inward focus on a feeling of being or having "less than" is not conducive to attracting abundance.

While everyone has moments of jealousy from time to time, if you find jealous feelings consume your thoughts, then this is an issue you're supposed to be working on in this life. If you're never truly happy when someone else has something good happen to them, you have an issue with jealousy. When your friend gets a new car, new house, new job, new love, do you feel resentful and consumed with the desire to have the same? Or can you truly say to yourself that you are deep down happy for them?

We all may feel envious of someone's success, while still feeling happy for that person. But if you don't feel happy for them, and wish you were the only one who success was granted to, then you need to work on the jealousy issue.

While you can feel jealousy over any number of things, the root cause is the same. You're wanting what someone else has, whether it's attention, money, a boyfriend, etc. It's that little person down inside you that questions your own worth, and always wants visual props to show that you are worthy. The lower your self- worth is, the more jealousy you feel for others who have what you *think* would make your self-worth higher.

Jealousy is one of the least comfortable emotions. Sadness even feels better than jealousy does. Sadness doesn't have hooks and barbs in it. Jealousy feels like anxiety laced with indignation and outrage. In fact, rage always seems to lie just below the surface of extremely jealous individuals. It's an angry emotion. Jealousy is confrontational and aggressive, requiring a lot of energy. Spending time around a *sad* person may drain your own energy, but it doesn't exhaust you the way being with a *jealous* person does. Jealousy saps everyone's energy, and damages relationships for the jealous person. In point, no one wants to be around them. So it only adds to their burden of feeling unworthy and unrewarded. People with major jealousy issues lose friends and lovers as quickly as they make them. They alienate people.

And what may come as the most shocking news to people who struggle with a lot of internal jealousy is the fact that it is *externally* transparent to everyone. Jealousy is always a thinly veiled emotion, because those hooks and barbs invariably poke through the veil. So while you may think you hide it well, you don't. You may fool yourself into believing you hide your jealousy with anger, sarcasm, haughtiness, or snobbery. You don't. The people affected by your jealousy are keenly aware of the problem, which should only exacerbate your jealous feelings. None of us ever wants to admit to feeling inadequate or inferior. It's hard enough to admit it to yourself, much less to a person you're feeling inferior to. That bitch.

Jealousy can drive people to focus on the object of their jealousy to the point of obsession. Here's a prime example:

> Karen is a highly successful corporate manager, and she possesses all the visible trappings of financial success. She has also been gifted with the physical beauty of a movie star, and she attracts men like flies. Upon first meeting, men see a beautiful, successful, independent woman. Men characteristically like to pursue women whose attention they have to work to get. So inevitably the chase ensues for this woman who appears to be self-possessed and full of self-confidence.

> Unfortunately for Karen, her suitors soon discover the defiantly jealous nature that resides at her core. Karen drives men away in droves. She called Terryee one day for advice on her latest pursuit.

> In hushed tones, Karen briefed Terryee on the man she feared was cheating on her. "I think he was overly nice to my secretary. He was full of compliments because she's lost a lot of weight. I was wearing a five hundred dollar dress, and he went on and on about how great she looked in this K-Mart special. Does he think I just wake up looking good in the morning? Doesn't he know how much time and money I spend trying to look good for him? I think he's screwing her."

"So your boyfriend was trying to give your secretary kudos for sticking to her diet, and suddenly he's sleeping with her?" Terryee asked.

"Well, I haven't caught them yet. But I broke into his house when I knew he was out of town and I snooped through everything I could find. I couldn't find anything suspicious. At least, not yet," Karen whispered.

"You broke into his house? And why are you whispering?" Terryee asked.

"I'm hiding in the bushes across the street. I want to see if he comes home with somebody."

While it was amusing to picture this highly successful woman crouching in someone's hedges to spy in her designer clothes, it was sad to see someone whose jealousy was eroding their own self-worth to that extent. Karen herself was ashamed and seeking help to conquer the demons that drove her to exhibit the clingy, desperate behavior of a stalker.

"Karen," Terryee admonished, "Get in your car and go home. Now!"

Terryee began working with Karen on finding her own value. She had become so dependent on the approval of others; she feared being viewed as 'not good enough' if someone else got a compliment instead of her. Karen felt driven to be the center of everyone's admiration. She became consumed with jealousy if she was not the sole recipient of her partner's attention. After months of working on her own self-worth meditations, Karen is now enjoying a new relationship. She recently told Terryee, "It's the first time I've just enjoyed being with a man without worrying. I'm just enjoying every moment as it comes."

Entitlement

Do you feel you have a right to something that others shouldn't get? Do you mentally justify why you deserve something more than other people do, even though you haven't actually worked for it more than they have?

There are many different versions of entitlement; familial "birthright" to inheritances or privileges, racial entitlement to special breaks, job entitlement based on age or longevity, parents who feel a sense of martyrdom entitlement, and spoiled brats of any age. People can always find a stupid reason to think they're entitled to something.

The problem with entitlement is not just the fact that everyone else thinks you're a lazy sponge, although that doesn't help your self-esteem when you have no friends. The problem is when you believe you deserve to be given things without having to do the work for them, you stop doing the work that will help you succeed and feel worthwhile. You can't really feel good about yourself as a human being when you're just waiting for the handouts that are coming your way because of your entitled designation. And, as many "entitled" people have discovered, just because *they* think they're entitled to special privileges or property, doesn't mean everyone else thinks that, and often they don't receive the things they believe they're entitled to. When the entitled person doesn't get what they want, they get very angry and indignant. Instead of spending their energy doing something constructive to work toward their goals, they just waste time being angry and looking for their next handout.

How 'bout those spoiled little rich kids? How many of them grow up to be unproductive members of society, hooked on drugs, blasting their parent's money on expensive hobbies and toys, and ultimately struggling with depression? I blame the parents for not instilling better values in their children. If you're telling your kid he deserves more – or better - than everyone else just because he's *your* kid, you're not giving him a sense of worthiness as an individual. He only sees his value to society as being the bearer of your name, instead of defining his own character and sharing his own gifts with the world.

People who struggle with entitlement are usually stuck in a constant feeling of *lack*. They're never getting as much as they think they deserve, so they're never coming from a feeling of positive abundance. And often they're lazy and unmotivated. They're not taking steps to get what they want because they believe the world should just hand it to them, so they regularly fail to realize their dreams.

Are you fond of saying some of these expressions?

> *He shouldn't have gotten that.*

> *She didn't deserve that.*

> *That was supposed to be mine.*

> *They didn't have any right to that.*

> *I'll be so pissed if they give it to him.*

> *I deserved that.*

> *They were not entitled to that.*

Of course, we all say those kinds of things once in a while, when we really feel someone is getting something they didn't work for. But if you regularly throw some of those expressions into your speech, you have some serious work to do on your entitlement issues. I'm not saying you're an ass. But I bet other people are.

Victimhood

Everyone loves a victim. Or at least, everyone *knows* a victim. They believe the whole world is against them, and everything bad just happens *to* them. They don't see themselves as an active participant in their own life. They struggle to take ownership. If you make a habit of pointing fingers instead of owning up to your participation when something goes wrong in your life, then you have a victim mentality.

If your loved ones often make jokes about you being "such a victim," this is the issue you're projecting. Victimhood keeps you stuck in that helpless, hopeless feeling. You don't feel like you have the ability to create the life you want, since life just happens *to* you. You often feel picked on or passed over. You don't believe good things are coming your way because, of course, "nothing good *ever* happens to *you*." You view yourself as the insignificant person who life just takes a dump on. If you have issues, it's because someone else caused them. Just as you blame others for your problems, you fail to take ownership of fixing them. We'll put that V on your forehead for you.

Victims are often underachievers. They prefer to wallow in the bottom of the self-pity pool, accepting whatever crumbs that happen to make it down to them, but never rising up to the surface to scavenge their own food. They don't feel they are capable of creating their own happiness, so they don't. Victims are usually miserable on the inside, although they may be very kind and friendly towards others.

> "Everyone keeps telling me I should apply for that job that's opening up in another division," Joe told me.

> "Cool! It sounds like a great promotion for you, and you'd be doing the kind of work you love to do," I encouraged.

"Yeah, but I don't think I'm going to. I don't think the supervisor over there likes me, and I would get so much work dumped on me. Even if I apply for it, I probably wouldn't get it anyway. That's my luck. I'd spend hours going through their interview process and still be stuck in my old job. I don't think they want me to get promoted in spite of all the stuff that I do. I think they'd rather just keep me down so they can use me to dump all the work on." Joe had already convinced himself not try for a better job, in spite of the fact that others were encouraging him.

Victimhood is the anti-serum to self-confidence. You don't believe you have the power to change your situation. You feel powerless to create your own happiness.

Do you frequently blame your parents, your ex, your siblings, friends, or co-workers for your misery or your failure to succeed? If you often say some of these things, you need to deal with your victim mentality:

My parents screwed me over....

My ex ruined me....

My boss hates me no matter what I do....

Of course, I'm the only one that didn't get....

I'm just waiting for the other shoe to drop....

Or, maybe you're right and the world just shits on you.

Anger

We all feel angry at times, but there are some people who have a constant feeling of nagging hostility *most* of the time. They're angry at their family, angry at their boss, co-workers, and friends for one reason or another. Passive-aggression is low-level anger. There's a simmering hostility beneath the surface. You may feel angry because of some of the other self-worth busters we've listed. Anger often accompanies entitlement, jealousy, and greed. Even the victims can be angry, because naturally, they've been victimized!

Anger is one of the strongest negative emotions, so it's an antithesis to positive thought. Anger draws you down into yourself and then explodes outward onto everyone around you. In passive aggressive anger, it's not so much an explosion as a stealthy form of hostility that destroys your relationships.

> "Diane! I'm so pissed at my wife! She told her family we'd be having Christmas with them. I hate those people! I can't even focus on work I'm so pissed!" Todd exploded.

> "Didn't you tell her last year that you would spend this holiday with her family?" I inquired.

> "Yes, but I'm overloaded at work and my assistant just stomped out on me because she said I'm mean! She says I yell too much! Effing prick!" Todd yelled.

27

"Todd, you need to take a breath and look at this from your wife's perspective, instead of getting angry at her. You promised a year ago that you would spend the holidays with her family. I remember she said it had been years since you'd made that concession. She's always too afraid to ask you to visit her folks for fear you'll get angry. Now you're proving her right. Why do you think your assistant walked out? Because you're always raising your voice in anger," I explained.

"I do not yell!" Todd yelled louder.

"You're yelling right now, you effing prick!" I yelled back.

Nobody enjoys being around someone who is angry, and the angry person drives people away. Spouses tip-toe around them, kids try to slip into the house undetected for fear of being yelled out, co-workers avoid the angry person's scorn, and the avoidance from others only makes the angry person angrier. They don't allow themselves to see the positives. They don't fully enjoy the love from people around them. It's almost like a shield in front of their body that deflects positive emotions from entering it. Negativity only draws in more negativity, and the angry person is always mad at the world and unhappy.

I won't give any examples of questions to ask yourself to determine if you're an angry person. You might get mad and yell at me, or rip up this nice book.

Greed

Greedy people always want more than they need. They are living in a continual state of lack, because they always feel they have to have more. Enough is never enough for them. They need more of everything. Regardless of how hefty their bank account is, they feel the need for more. They don't ever have enough material possessions, in *their* mind. No matter how much they have, they don't have enough to suit them. They don't enjoy their one or two pieces of the pie. They're not happy unless they have the whole pie and there's none left for anyone else. But they're not satisfied if everyone lets them have the whole pie, just to shut them up. They demand another pie. They're pie hogs.

Greedy people suck. They suck the positive vibes out of everyone else. They're never happy to let you enjoy your own pie piece. They're hovering over you while you're eating it, and you finally just say, "Hey do you want to eat the rest of this for me, asshole?"

Greedy people have difficulty maintaining close relationships because they usually alienate everyone they've tried to take things from in their haste to get more.

If you feel you never have enough and you want everyone else's share, you'll never get out of your state of "wanting" until you deal with your greed issues.

Covetousness

Covetousness is the first cousin of Jealousy. As described by Webster's: Coveting is to feel blameworthy desire for that which is another's; excessively desiring the possessions of another. The word 'coveting' is most often used to describe an intense desire for material items, but you can covet anything from an object to a person to an idea. Essentially, it's a form of jealousy that becomes focused on particular items or people.

If you find yourself continually thinking about attainment of something that belongs to another, you're having an issue with coveting. If you think possession of that item would bring you joy, you're wrong. It might give you temporary satisfaction the moment you possessed it, but you would soon find something else to covet, and once again, feel unsatisfied with the lack of having it.

According to The Law of Attraction, we will always feel lacking when we are always focused on our lack of having. We will never attract abundance in our lives when we are focused on lack. We attract what we put out. Covetousness is a prime example of The Law of Attraction at work. People who struggle with this issue are never happy and content with what they have. They spend their lives in a continual state of jealous 'wanting.' Their feeling of lack attracts more lack.

While no one wants to admit they are guilty of this, we all know if we struggle with it, even if others are not aware. The point is, if you are covetous, you are never really happy. This book is intended to help you find peace within yourself, so shake off the denial and keep reading.

Jealousy and Covetousness both stem from a lack of contentment within. You think, "If I only had that job or that spouse or that car, I would be happy." You're always looking outside yourself for that one 'thing' that will make you happy, instead of looking within. You assume another person is happy just because they are the owner of that car, that job, or that life. In truth, happy people are happy because they see their own self-worth. Their cars, jobs, or spouses don't give them their self-esteem. *They* do. But very often, their self-esteem has gotten them their spouses and jobs!

We most often associate coveting with material objects, but we can also covet people, as evidenced by the next client. She takes the idea of "wanting it all" to a whole new level.

> Cindy was a married woman who was having an affair with a single man in her office, George. In her initial phone call to Terryee, she was asking for a reading on this relationship. Cindy wanted to know if George really loved her, and if Terryee saw a future for her with this man.

31

Terryee asked Cindy, "Are you prepared to leave your husband for this other man?"

"No. I just want to know if he loves me."

Terryee said, "The question is, do you love him or your husband? Because I'm not seeing a love connection between you and this new guy."

Cindy replied, "I think I love them both. My husband is my husband. I'm *married* to him, and I don't want a divorce. He's a good man. But George gives me a lot of attention and he makes me laugh and I love the way I feel when we have sex."

Terryee tried switching gears, "Let me explain something to you. When you really love someone, you love things about them that are unrelated to you. For example, you love the way they treat their family, or you love the sound of their laugh, or you love the way their hands move across the piano keys, or you love the way they always make shy people feel included in conversations.......you see what I mean? When you say you love the things they do for you to make *you* feel good, that's really a selfish attachment. You're not saying you love George. You're saying you love the attention. You love the feeling of being the center of his attention. You're looking to him to fill a void inside you. You're not really loving George. Do you feel your husband does not give you enough attention?"

"Oh, he tries, but it's hard with our kids and jobs and everything. But he always does nice things for me and the kids. He's a great dad and I know I can count on him."

Terryee's hope that Cindy would start reflecting on her own motives was dashed in a subsequent phone call.

"He's engaged!" wailed Cindy. "George got engaged and he broke it off with me!"

"Okay, let me ask you this again. Were you planning on leaving your husband for George?" Terryee inquired.

"No. But I don't want George to get married. Is there something I can do to stop this marriage from happening? I mean, like a spell or something?" Cindy asked.

"I don't do spells. I'm not a witch, although some men I've dated might argue that point," Terryee joked. "So you're telling me, you don't want to leave your husband for George, but you don't want George to find happiness with someone who is available to him."

"Yes. Can you help me?"

Needless to say, Cindy did not get the kind of help that she initially asked for. Terryee really needs to brush up on those spells. Doesn't everyone need a good witch now and then? Hopefully George found happiness with someone who truly loved him instead of coveting men and attention. Cindy's husband is in our prayers, while Cindy still struggles with the meaning of love. Angels can't fix stupid.

Manifesting Abundance

While we could continue to list different qualities that erode self-worth, they are all inevitably stemming from fear: Lying, Martyrdom, Snobbery, and the list goes on. It's important for everyone to look at themselves objectively to determine where their own greatest fears lie, and how this fear causes them to respond. To master the art of creating your dreams through positive thought, a different response is required. Love needs to shine where fear lies in the shadows. Optimism must reign over negativity. So how do you get there? No, put the vodka back down.

First you make a list of things you desire. Everyone has their own unique list, but some common desires are financial freedom, romantic love, cars, houses, babies, you name it. But instead of writing "car, money, house, love....," write the words, "I am buying my new car," or "I am enjoying my new house," or "I have X amount of dollars in my savings account and I don't have any debts." Write your own list as if you already have these things.

As our friend Chris said, "I own a silver Jaguar. I don't have it in the driveway right now, but there's a Jaguar out there that belongs to me. I already have it because I *believe* I have it, so I know it's coming to me."

After you have made your list, then what? Do as the athletes do: visualize. Sit down in a quiet place and visualize yourself living the life you want. If you desire a partner, visualize sharing your life with that person. Make your visualizations detailed. Picture the house you want to live in. Where is it? What does your living room look like? What words would you like to share with your loved one? What activities are you enjoying together? What is your dream job? Imagine being in the perfect life of your dreams, enjoying all the items on the list you created, and feel the negativity lift away from you as you fantasize about living the dream. When you get to a point of feeling serene and joyful, you're in a state of higher vibration. Your mood is lighter and happier and peaceful. This is the mood you want to be in when you focus on your intentions.

You want to come from a place of positivity and love, instead of negativity and fear. If you are coming from fear, you are essentially pushing away the dream. If you fear you won't achieve it, the universe will give you back what you expect. Fearing is akin to believing, in the law of attraction principles. With that in mind, it may be easier to look at it from the reverse perspective. If the universe delivers what you expect it to, then expect the best and it will be delivered to you.

As you sit there in your peaceful reverie fantasizing about your dream life, focus your thoughts on believing it all will be yours. It may be easier to concentrate on your list if you read it aloud, but you can read it silently if you feel awkward or embarrassed to verbally recite affirmations. Add anything you desire to the visualization and accompanying mantra, and be as clear and detailed as possible. If you want a blue house, then make sure you say blue. If you want to retire and start your own business, then make sure you stipulate what kind of a business it is. If you want a partner who enjoys sex five times a day, make sure you are clear on the sex thing.

While this may feel awkward to you at first, you will begin to enjoy your meditation time. Sometimes it's the only way to force yourself to have some quiet time alone! However you choose to study your own meditation is fine, as long as your mind is focused on the words and your intentions, and you are coming from a positive state of mind.

After you have repeated your meditation numerous times, it will become ingrained in your memory. Terryee has helped me write my own meditations, and I ponder them at different times throughout the day; silently meditating on each one while I do other tasks. It keeps my goals fresh in my mind as I deal with the daily hustle and bustle. I liken it to the Marine's mantra, "I will not fail." If you keep focusing on your own personal affirmations, they become part of who you are. You begin believing them. You envision yourself achieving the manifestation that has become ingrained in your mind.

There are so many stories from people who have successfully used the law of attraction to achieve their dreams. Terryee recently got a call from a client she had mentored a year earlier.

"Hello, Terryee? This is Bob. I'm in St. Lucia."

"Bob?" Terryee took a moment to register which Bob would be in St. Lucia.

"Yeah, remember a year ago I was out of work and I told you I wanted to land a job that I could use my artistic talents in, and I wanted to meet my dream girl and get married in the Caribbean?"

"Yes!" memory jogged. "How are you, Bob?"

"Well, I'm calling to tell you I landed a job I love, met the greatest lady in the world, and I am here in St. Lucia to get married tomorrow! It worked for me. The manifesting. The law of attraction. All the things you helped me work on. I'm livin' the dream!"

Bob is not the only success story, but he's the only one we know who went to the Caribbean Islands to tie the knot.

Cellular Memory

The concept of cellular memory has been debated amongst medical researchers, primarily stemming from the experiences of organ transplant victims. A woman who hated sports suddenly lives and breathes for football, after receiving an organ from a young man who loved the game. Favorite tastes, colors, and textures of transplant recipients reportedly changed to those of their organ donors, without prior knowledge of the donor's history, personality, or tastes. Is it possible that cells carry a memory of their own?

Feelings come before thoughts. When you hear a song on the radio that you associate with another time in your life, you actually feel the emotions surrounding that memory before your mind generates the thought of it. It's similar to the way intuition precedes rational thought. When you meet someone, your intuition usually tells you right away if that person will inevitably hurt you. But in a split second, your mind makes a decision to disregard that subtle warning and enter into a relationship with that person, because your eyes like the looks of it, and your mind chatter drowns out that little voice of warning.

But while cellular memory and intuitive feelings both come before thoughts do, the similarities between the two stop there. Memory stems from perception of prior experience. Intuition arises from a sense of *knowing* truth. While your memories are your true recollection of past experiences, they are based on *your* perception of the experience. We know our perception is not always an accurate portrait of actual happenings. Yet our minds will attach negative meaning to words and sounds from an earlier situation that felt painful to us. The feelings associated with certain words will cloud our intention before the thought of that word actually enters our mind.

The word *wealthy* is a good example. For some, *wealthy* conjures up a negative image of snobbery and materialism, with greed often accompanying it. Most of us have been programmed with the puritanical belief that "it is harder for a rich man to get into heaven than a poor man." So if we tell ourselves we are manifesting *wealth* in our life, we have immediately sabotaged the desire to acquire financial freedom if we also desire an entrance into heaven. It's very important to choose words that do not have a negative connotation in our memory. Feeling comes before thought. Remember that before you speak. Choose words that do not have negative thoughts or fears attached to them.

If you grew up in a household where money was always an issue, and fear surrounded every discussion you overheard regarding *money,* do not include the word *money* in your manifesting. One word with negative or fearful attachments will change your desire for abundance into a *fear* of it.

Money is not a bad thing. God put all things on this earth for us to enjoy as long as we place higher value on the truly important intangibles that come from God. Love, compassion, kindness, and benevolence are God qualities. Charity and benevolence do not have negative connotations, and yet money is frequently attached to them. So if you desire financial wealth, why not say, "I am acquiring financial abundance that will allow me to live in freedom while helping many others through my own benevolence." If you have a specific fear attached to the words abundance, freedom or benevolence, choose different words that feel positive to you.

It's so important to make sure you are not coming from *fear* or *lack* when you are working on your own manifesting. We are giving you some examples of mantras to use while meditating or contemplating your goals. You can alter them any way you like to make them personal. We call these mantras *I am's,* but you do not have to start every sentence with the words "I am." You just need to make sure you are not saying, "I want," or "I wish," or "I hope," as these words actually focus on your current *lack* of something you desire, rather than the attainment of it. If you are coming from a state of lack, you will receive the lack of what you desire in return.

I am acquiring financial freedom.

I am experiencing unconditional love with the man/woman of my dreams.

I am healthy and fit.

I am enjoying the career I love.

I am buying the home/car/hairdryer of my dreams.

I have abundance in all areas of my life.

I am free of addictions.

I am worthy of love and success.

I am sexy and beautiful.

Cellular memory is different from your subconscious mind, but both can initiate self-sabotaging behavior. Your subconscious mind always works to create whatever your conscious mind believes will happen. Your subconscious doesn't bring in its own objectives. It simply works to make sure the beliefs that are held in the conscious brain are confirmed. So even if you're saying you desire success in love or money, if you don't truly believe in your own ability to attain it, you are basically giving your subconscious mind a direct order to prohibit you from attaining your goals. We sabotage ourselves when we don't believe in our own ability to prosper.

Dr. Joseph Murphy made a great contribution towards unlocking this mystery for us in his book, **The Power of Your Subconscious Mind.** He explains how people have learned to control their own subconscious thought in order to create desired outcomes. Some have gone as far as healing themselves of physical ailments that medicine could not cure.

We know several people who have cured themselves of severe physical ailments, and Terryee is a prime example. Terryee actually healed herself from a diabetic health crisis. After being hospitalized due to complications from her diabetes, including blindness, Terryee enlisted the help of a nutritionist and began her own recovery program using the principles outlined in this book. She worked on daily meditations while nurturing her body back to health, and proved to herself that 'mind over matter' is possible. While we are certainly not advocating a discontinuance of any medications, we are suggesting a daily ritual of positive affirmations will hasten recovery, at the least.

Heidi Hoke is a friend of ours, and she's got an amazing story. She landed in the hospital suffering between 10-12 grand mal epileptic seizures a day. She also had fibromyalgia, Tourette's syndrome, and bi-polar disorder. The doctors tried a multitude of treatments, but nothing seemed to alleviate the seizures. Her neurologist suggested brain surgery.

During this time, Heidi lost everything. She could no longer work to support herself, and her kids had to go stay with family. Heidi was so incapacitated; she had to use extreme focus and determination to simply get one of her fingers to move. But she didn't want the brain surgery. Heavily medicated, Heidi finally left the hospital, determined to find another solution to her problem. She bought one book on natural healing methods, and began treating herself through natural means. Flash forward to today; Heidi is on her way to earning *two* doctorates. She's a scientist, and Heidi frequently tells us, "The brain is a powerhouse."

As with eastern medicine, the ability to manifest successfully requires a holistic approach. The whole body, mind, and spirit must be taken into account, and essentially re-trained in thought and belief. If cells have a memory of their own, different pathways need to be developed in order to bypass negative information being fed to your brain.

One woman had been a victim of childhood molestation by her father. During those encounters, he frequently told her she was being a "good girl." Those words became ingrained in her psyche to the point of invoking severe stomach pains and nausea whenever she heard them. The feelings surrounding those words were much stronger than any cognitive thoughts that followed. She had difficulty explaining to her husband why she was experiencing severe mood swings after they adopted a new puppy, since she had kept many of her painful memories a secret. But once informed, her husband was quite relieved to learn her wrath was not aimed at him or the puppy, but rather the phrase he kept using while training their female beagle. "Good girl." They decided upon a new phrase together, "Smart dog!"

The story above is an extreme example of negative feelings attached to words, but even less traumatic memories can be just as powerful in attaching negativity onto something else. Perhaps you struggled with many headaches when buying your first house. Many of us have come to feel a slight sense of dread when we hear the words "new house," depending on our own experiences. So if you desire to move into a more lavish setting, choose words that feel good to you. "I am purchasing the home of my dreams." Visualize yourself inside your dream home, and feel the satisfaction and contentment you will feel when you're snuggled inside. That warm contented feeling is the place you need to come from when you're repeating your mantra, "I am purchasing the home of my dreams." Feel the contentment and peace before you speak the words. Choose words that maintain that feeling.

If you are manifesting a great love relationship, take a moment to imagine how you will feel when your chosen partner is showering you with affection, which you are returning to them. Imagine feeling completely and unconditionally loved, safe, and secure with your soul mate. Sink into that blissful feeling and hold onto it while you meditate on your intentions. "I am experiencing unconditional love with my soul mate." It's so important that you are coming from a loving place of abundance when you are manifesting.

If you're feeling angry or jealous when you're focusing on your intentions for love, you will sabotage your own efforts. You *must* be coming from a positive, loving state of mind to attract a positive, loving relationship into your life. Focus your intentions on the feelings of abundance you desire, and then choose words that mimic that feeling for you.

The Art of Allowing

You've been given an overall summary of the Law of Attraction in the previous chapter, but we want to discuss a couple of points in detail. While the first step is training your mind to elevate to a positive level of thinking, the next step is *allowing* yourself to receive the positive vibrations from the universe. The Art of Allowing is the ability to remove the mental and emotional roadblocks that prohibit you from maintaining positive expectations.

Here's a perfect example of someone who is 'thinking positive,' but still letting deep-seated fears block their own success:

"Hello, Terryee? This is Tom."

"Hi Tom! How is everything going with your girlfriend?"

"Great! I think. Here's my question. We're talking about taking this one step further, and she's going to move in with me whenever she can find a job that's close to where my house is. She agrees that it just makes sense for *her* to move, since she's just renting an apartment in Seattle and I own my house in Los Angeles. You know this is what I've hoped and prayed for. I've spent hours working with the meditations you helped me create to manifest a closer relationship with her, as well as prosperity in my career. My new job is going great, and I'm making a lot more money. So my question is, when do you think she will move here?" Tom asked.

"Whenever you *allow* her to," Terryee answered. "You're letting your old fears prohibit you from taking that step. What's stopping her from moving right now? You are. You are letting your fear of money stop you from getting the girl of your dreams. You are now making more than enough money to support *both* of you if she leaves her job now and moves in with you before she finds another job. If you call her up and suggest that she just pack up and move right now, what do you think she will say?"

"I think she'd say yes," Tom replied.

"So why are you asking *me* when she will move in with you? She'll move *now* if you allow it to happen. The better question is, when will *you* allow it? How much income do you think a two person household needs to get by for the short time it would take a woman with two degrees to find a job in a large metropolitan area?"

Tom laughed, "Good point."

"How much money do you need to see in your bank account before you will think you can afford to feed a tiny woman who hardly eats for a month or so? You're blocking yourself from getting what you want. You want her to live with you. You need to take a look at these old fears and ask yourself why they are still controlling you. Maybe you need to write a new meditation that says, 'I am having sex every night,'" Terryee laughed. "Do you think *that* would help?"

"I'm on it!" Tom signed off.

Tom had used positive affirmations and positive thinking to attract the woman of his dreams into his life and secure a much higher paying job. Money was important to him. It was also a fear of his. Fear of *lack* of money. He always put money as an obstacle in his own way, even if it wasn't an issue. Tom had made it all the way around the track, but fear was not allowing him to take the last stride across the finish line. Mentally, he wasn't allowing the universe to bring him all the goodies it had to offer.

The key to allowing life to bring you what you desire is the ability to stop letting past issues hold you back. Some issues are so deeply imbedded in our psyche; we don't even realize they exist.

I realized I had not been practicing what I preach after two different dreams I had on consecutive nights. On the first night, I dreamed I lived in a room of a boarding house, and my ex-boyfriend lived across the hall with his new girlfriend. The new girlfriend did not like me, and was making it difficult for me and the man to clean out the old furniture and boxes we had accumulated together.

The second night, I dreamed I lived in the basement of the same boarding house with my ex-boyfriend, and we were back together again. This time, I was cleaning out old boxes and furniture that my ex-husband and I had accumulated from our 20 year marriage.

When I began analyzing these two dreams, I realized I had old emotional garbage from my marriage that had affected my relationship with my ex-boyfriend. Although the two men were totally different in personality and emotional complexities, I had the same issue with both of them. It was *my* issue. It had nothing to do with the men. I had allowed my feelings to be treated with disregard in almost every romantic relationship I'd had since I'd gotten divorced. My ex-husband never mistreated my feelings, but I had rarely surfaced them with him if I was hurt. It's important to remember here, it's not the men's fault. I'm the one who *allowed* my feelings to be treated as 'not as important' as others. I also realized, my ex-husband had never meant to make me feel unimportant, but it was my own dim view of myself combined with the dominating presence of my mother-in-law that caused me to believe this. So when my own self-worth issues from my marriage started surfacing with my new boyfriend, I had continued the same pattern of behavior: shoving my own feelings under the rug. But I knew any mistreatment actually stemmed from me, as I was not treating my *own* feelings as if they were as important as my partner's. I had been 'a good sport' and acted in the role of the nurturer who always put my own feelings and desires on the back burner. I acted like I didn't care about things that actually hurt me. I viewed myself and my feelings as 'not important.' And you always get what you believe you'll get. The only thing the men were guilty of: believing my acting job. I deserved an Oscar!

With a mountain of help from Terryee, I had done a lot of internal work on my self-worth issues since both of those relationships had ended, and yet I realized I was still repeating the same mistakes with different men. I found my own behavior to be confusing. I now *knew* I was worthy of real love, so why was I still not allowing it to happen?

After several false starts with different men, I finally realized I would keep repeating the same behavior over and over until I learned how to allow myself a great love with an attentive partner. The problem was not in finding a man who would put my needs on the same level as his. The problem was in making *me* put my needs on the same level as my partner's. If you don't put yourself on an equal playing field with your partner, then don't expect them to either.

Part of my meditation for healing the part of me that wouldn't allow the kind of love I desired was channeled through Terryee. Terryee was given a prayer from Archangel Chamuel, and I began repeating it daily. You can substitute Jesus, God, Buddha, The Blessed Mother, or whomever you pray to; or eliminate any words you do not feel comfortable with or necessary. The important thing to remember when you are saying prayers and mantras is that you need to feel comfortable with the terminology. When I invoke a particular angel in a prayer, I usually just direct the prayer to that angel specifically. Other people prefer praying to many different spiritual beings with one prayer, so I am including the whole list that Terryee was given. I admit to shortening it myself and directing it to Chamuel alone.

> Thank you Archangel Chamuel and all angels, ascended masters, and the great "I am" (God), for bringing me this great romantic relationship. As he or she has been prepared to be with me, I have been prepared for him or her. Thank you for bringing this to me. Thank you for prepared healing, balancing karma, and most of all allowing. Thank you for bringing us together in divine and perfect timing. I am your holy child and I am ready to accept and receive this relationship.

You can write out this prayer in shortened version for yourself, and keep it with you. I began looking at it and reading it throughout the day, and every time I recited it, silently or aloud, I would feel a sense of excitement. Believing that great love is going to come your way *should* leave you feeling excited! But sometimes you need a little push to get onto that higher vibrational wave length of excited expectancy. This prayer worked for me, because the words are essentially saying, "Thank you for giving me this. I believe you are working to bring me this and it's coming to me." Whereas our usual prayers for assistance sound more like, "Pleeeeez can I have this? I really *want* this. I really *hope* I get this...." And as discussed in previous chapters, the words *want* and *hope* are words coming from a state of lack, so lack is what we get.

The prayer is also helpful in lifting the feeling of being stuck in-waiting, in a pause moment, where time is just not moving fast enough. If you look at your future partner as currently in the process of 'being prepared' to love you unconditionally, then you can withstand the wait more patiently. You don't want them until they are ready! You also must look at yourself as 'being prepared' to love them unconditionally, and you do not want your soul mate to appear before you are ready yourself. By saying, "I am ready," you will bring them to you sooner.

Another common mistake that blocks you from meeting the right partner is the unwillingness to let go of the wrong partner. Many people get stuck in this rut. They don't want to let go of a 'sure thing' unless they have another 'sure thing' lined up and waiting in the wings. Love doesn't work like that – at least, not usually. When you cling to someone who isn't right for you out of fear that no one else will come along, you are in essence blocking the right person from coming in. You must be willing to let go and trust that you are worthy of the right person's love and the universe will send you the right person when you are finally free and able to accept them.

It sounds cliché, but you must stop living in the past and feel joy in the current moment, in order to manifest the abundance you want in the future. Focused intention on celebrating the joy in the present will draw joy into your future. Prayers and mantras are an easy way to draw your mind into focus on being thankful for the things you *do* have, rather than the things you lack. Repetition throughout the day will give your thoughts and feelings buoyancy, and help you refrain from getting bogged back down into depressing, negative thinking.

The Art of Allowing is all about focus. Focus is a force. If you focus on the past, you are bringing the past negativity into your present, and sabotaging your future. Continued thoughts of past hurts only allow them to cause you more pain in the present, and you bring it right on into your future. Focusing on positive, loving, abundant aspects of your life will bring more of the same.

When you think you are focused on the love, career, and life of your dreams, why is there a delay in getting them? It's always inside you. As soon as you release your blocks, the future you want will come to you. So it's always important to look internally for old issues that still may be interfering with your current state of mind. Old memories or old grudges that you haven't resolved may be holding you back.

When I realized I still had a lot of old negativity inside of me, I checked out of the dating game for a while to work on myself. Knowing I would eventually get back out into the social scene when I was ready, I took over a year to address my own issues and work on resolving them. That may seem like a long time to some people, but most middle-aged people can look back on their past year and think it flew by. Not only did it fly by, but their situation hasn't changed much from the previous year. That's okay if they didn't want it to change, but a lot of them do. Yet, they did nothing to facilitate any changes, because it was easier to be lazy in their routine.

While Terryee and I are not advocating becoming a recluse for a year, we're saying that your dreams may not be manifesting if there is an emotional block inside of you, holding you back. And until you address that issue, it will continue doing so. When you start concentrating on yourself, there is nothing you can't do. (And no, it won't take you a year!)

Unfortunately, you will not attract the love of your dreams until you feel happy by yourself. That is the crux of the matter. You are not *lacking* a soul mate. You must learn to love yourself before you will be gifted with a perfect match. When you are 'searching' for a soul mate, the word 'search' implies that something is missing, and you need to look for it. Nothing is missing. You desire a soul mate, but you are complete unto yourself. If you're wearing holes in your carpet, pacing the floor because you're overwhelmed with anxiety of being by yourself, then you are not ready for a real love relationship with another person. You have to learn to love yourself first. Once you do, then you have to allow yourself happiness and fulfillment. Some people find one thing harder than the other.

I found it easier to love myself, but struggled with the allowing part. Others struggle to love themselves for years, but once they do, allowing themselves happiness seems to come in conjunction with loving themselves. We all take different paths to happiness.

Keeping your focus on the goals you have for yourself is difficult, and that's another roadblock we all encounter. Sometimes there are so many opportunities, so many variables, so many 'what ifs' and so many varieties of candy in the candy store. When you are faced with making a decision, part of making a choice is in choosing to let go of the others. If you fail to do so, you may find yourself empty-handed in the end.

One of Terryee's clients feels 'stuck' in a relationship with someone she no longer desires. Judy has been in a long term relationship with a man who she believes may have a drug problem. They don't spend enough time together for her to determine if this is actually a problem, but she knows he has some sort of an emotional issue or addiction. Judy feels obligated to 'stand by him' now, but longs for a more meaningful connection with someone new.

> "Hi Terryee, this is Judy. I'm wondering if you think there is someone else out there for me, or should I stay with the man I'm with."

> "Judy, there is always someone else out there for you. Are you asking me if you would be happier with someone else? Sure. You think your guy has a drug problem, or some other issue that's making him keep you at arm's length, and you're not happy with that."

> "But I keep debating on whether I should stay with this one. I think he has a problem, and we're not getting closer to each other," Judy said.

> "Judy, you're holding onto this guy out of fear that you won't meet somebody else. That 'somebody else' isn't going to come to you when you're attached to this other man. If you're debating on staying with your guy because you really love him, then that's another story. Do you love him or do you just love the comfort of having a steady boyfriend? That's what you need to ask yourself. If this man started showing up and wanting to see you all the time, and you didn't think he had a drug problem, would you look at him and say to yourself, 'He's everything I want in a partner?' I've never heard you talk about any good

qualities that you really love about this man. Do I think there's someone better for you? Yes. Do I think you'll meet this new man until you let go of the old one? No."

Judy is making the mistake we have all made at one time or another. Whether we make it with a partner, a job, a situation, a habit; if we tell ourselves we'll let go of the old when the new comes to us, we're going to sit there being stuck in our old situation forever. It takes courage and a lot of self-love to make changes in our lives. Sometimes we're on the fence about whether they are positive or negative changes. But you only need to listen to your heart and follow your intuition to know if they are changes which are right for you. If you dream of being with a different partner, then you need to let go of your current partner. If you dream of being in a different line of work, then your current job is not the right one for you, no matter how much money you're making. But, yeah, you better look for another job before you quit.

If you hate your job and you're sitting there waiting for the perfect opportunity to fall in your lap, you'll be waiting until you get fired. We've all seen it happen to others we work with, even if it hasn't happened to us. When people get stuck in a situation that no longer brings them joy and excitement, they mentally check out. They may feel like they're still putting their nose to the grindstone every day, but emotionally, they don't have that fire in their belly anymore. They're bored, tired, stuck in a routine. Though their job may be challenging, if they hate it, they're tired of the challenges. They get a knot in their stomach when they even think about having to go in to work. But they tell themselves they 'need' the paycheck, and they feel more comfortable staying stuck in their routine. So why can't they progress to the next step? Because, they have their own mental blocks that do not allow them to believe in their own ability to succeed. They are afraid to try something different out of fear of failure. So while they may visualize themselves in the perfect career, and attempt to use the Law of Attraction for attainment, they are still sabotaging themselves by not getting to the root of the issue that prohibits them from allowing themselves to attain their desires.

It's a two-step process. The roadblocks are always on the inside; not on the outside.

Here's another example of a lady who is holding herself back. Her own issue is entitlement, rather than fear or low self-worth.

> Regina complained, "Terryee, I've been with this company for twenty years, and I'm tired of getting passed over! My family has struggled with racism since before I was born, and I know if I was a young white woman, I would have had that promotion. They just handed that job I wanted to a 28 year old white girl, because she's a total brown-noser. They told me she's got a Master's Degree and she had been taking night classes in Workers

59

Compensation Laws to make herself more qualified for the HR job, and since I haven't had any HR training, they awarded the job to her. She's more qualified? That's bull! I've been slaving away in this stupid clerical department for 20 years. I may not be trained on all the federal tax forms and laws, but they owed me a shot."

"Regina, I know I sound like the devil's advocate here, but was the posted job asking for someone with knowledge of HR tax forms and Workers Comp Laws?" Terryee inquired.

"Yes, but they could have trained me."

"Yes, but if they were looking for someone that didn't need to be trained, then I don't think they were actually discriminating against you or anyone else who didn't have that training. I wouldn't look at this as white versus black or young versus old. I would look at it as a learning experience for the job that you really want. If you really desire a job in Human Resources, then I would do what the 28 year old did, and go enroll yourself in some classes. Then, the next time there's an opening, you'll be qualified."

Regina may or may not have taken Terryee's advice. Sometimes when people have been working for a company for a long time, they feel the company 'owes them.' Regina believed she should have been given the job over someone who had taken the initiative to go back to school to meet the job's qualifications, just because she'd worked there longer.

When we feel entitled to something, we put up our own roadblock to getting that something. We frequently fail to see there are steps we need to take, or extra work we need to do to be awarded the thing we want. We think it should just be given to us, based on factors that do not actually pertain to the award we're wanting. Longevity at a company does not mean you're qualified to perform every task involved in the running of the company. Discrimination of any kind works both ways when you're talking about entitlement. So sometimes, allowing yourself to have something means you need to do some external work in order to get it. While this book is focused on the internal work, we also have a firm grip on the reality of business, as well as relationships. If there are obvious factors that will determine someone else's ability to *not* allow you to have something, work on eliminating them, instead of holding a grudge against that person or company. Don't be your own worst enemy.

Part of Allowing is the motivation to take baby steps. As our friend Heidi says, "No goal is too small." My friend, John, said, "If the only thing you do today is concentrate on *not* repeating the mistakes you've made in the past, then that's a step forward. You may not be doing anything to take a great stride forward, but as long as you don't repeat your old mistakes, then that's an advance."

The crucial part of the Art of Allowing is to eliminate any roadblocks that would prohibit you from getting what you desire. Those blocks may be emotional debris, mental negativity or cynicism, physical objects, fear, etc. When you know your path is free and clear to get what you want, and you know you deserve to have it, you will draw it to you with focused intentions.

Hanging onto the memory of an old love is one of the most common "blocks" people create for themselves. While they want a new love, and they say they're ready for one, they still secretly harbor the desire for the old one to come back. As long as they keep secretly wishing for the last person, a new person isn't going to step through the door. They've created an internal energy block. They think they're open to a new mate, but the hope they're still pinning onto their old mate is telling the universe, "This one's taken. They don't need a new partner. They're still clinging to their old partner's energy."

Deliberate Creation

To refresh our first two steps; you must first bring your own positive energy level up to match the positive vibrations you want to attract from the universe around you. Positive attracts positive. Next, you want to mentally remove any blocks you've created that inhibit desirable things from coming your way. Expect positive changes to happen, and allow the universe to bring them to you.

Now let's focus on your intentions. You must have a focused intent on the situations you wish to create for yourself. We call this deliberate creation. You are deliberately creating the life of your dreams.

When I first met Terryee, she shared the messages about my life that she was getting from my angels and guides. Some of those visions for my future sounded completely far-fetched, and I am thankful I had written them down during our first conversation. As things began happening as she had predicted, I became a firm believer in the messages she was receiving. I also had my own determination to create the life I envisioned for myself, in spite of hurdles and heartbreaks. I don't have clairvoyant abilities, but I believe in myself.

When I moved to Oklahoma after my kids had both graduated from college, it was with the belief that I had to move there in order for my son to follow and settle where he felt comfortable. Mikey had mild autism, also known as Asperger's Syndrome, and he never felt like he fit in with the more sophisticated kids in Denver, where he had grown up. I had moved with the belief that it was a fresh new start for me. I'd been divorced for several years and spinning my wheels in my job. So I took the opportunity to get a transfer to open a new store for the retail company I worked for, and forge the way for Mikey to move along behind me. It was very difficult leaving both my kids in Colorado at that time, but I believed it was all going to work out for all of us. I knew Mikey was joining me shortly, and my daughter, Susie, was toying with the idea.

Flash forward a couple of years. Mikey committed suicide in a Wal-Mart in Oklahoma after suffering a delusional episode. My world turned upside down. Twenty-five years of my life had been devoted to making his life better. And he ended it. I was heartbroken and rudderless. Prior to Mikey's death, I had been fussing a lot with my boyfriend of two years, and we broke up a month after Mikey died. A month after that, I unexpectedly met a man who I immediately felt was a soul mate. I fell madly in love with him, and I think it kept me afloat that first year without Mikey.

A year and a half later, I could feel this man was distancing himself from me. I believed the long hours I was working on the weekends were not helping the situation with him. Unhappy and stagnant in my job, I left the company I had been with for ten years and began a new job. Several days before I started my new job, the man I loved broke the news to me that someone else had entered the picture and he was struggling to make a decision to stay with me or not. I was devastated. Another loss.

Meanwhile, my daughter needed me in Colorado. She had been through hell herself. Losing her brother, skin cancer, numerous breakups, and I was seven hundred miles away. I had finished the manuscript for my first book, and I didn't even know where to begin in my quest for a publisher. I was depressed and miserable.

Six months later, I just woke up one day and said, 'I am moving back to Colorado.' I got it in my head that I was going to just pack up and start all over. But it wasn't a defeatist attitude. I had been talking to Terryee a lot about the power of intention and the law of attraction and deliberate creation. I knew if I had survived the last couple of years, I could do anything. So I wrote my own meditation that began, 'I am moving to Colorado. I am being offered a new job there. I am getting my book published.'

I repeated this multiple times every day. I didn't know how I was going to afford a cross-country move. I had no job in Colorado. I had no publisher in sight. But I *believed* I was going to do all those things.

I tearfully told my superiors that although I loved my new job, I needed to move back to Colorado. The company I worked for had a sister company in Denver, but they had never transferred managers between the two chains. Within several days, I had an offer from the human resources director to transfer me to a Denver branch of the other chain. They also paid for my moving expenses. Two weeks later, my furniture was packed and loaded and headed to Denver. My mom had spent the day with the furniture movers, since I was still working at my current store. I had to say goodbye to her that night, and she had been my rock after Mikey had died.

That was one of the hardest days of my life. Standing in that empty house...the last home I had shared with Mikey. The last time I had seen him alive was in that doorway. The last time I had seen the man I loved was in the same doorway. Both men; walking out that door, and out of my life.

The clouds were rolling in with thunderstorms in Oklahoma, and I knew there was a blizzard headed for Denver and I needed to get on the road. It was the end of January, and not the best weather for moving. I felt so empty and lost that day, standing in that empty house. I felt like I had lost *everything*. If I hadn't unwillingly lost it, I had given it up: my son, my love, my jobs, my homes. Even my nineteen year old cat had died that year. Kitty had been my best buddy for almost as long as my kids had been alive.

So I packed up my remaining buddy, the seventeen year old cat, Sneakers, and I strapped her carrier case into the front seat with me, right alongside the box that still held a small portion of Mikey's ashes. I had the back seat full of house plants that had been funeral arrangements two years earlier, and I carefully set a bouquet of dried roses atop them. The roses had been the first bouquet I had gotten from the man I still loved madly, and they were so sentimental to me, I couldn't bear to part with them yet.

Sometimes life just prunes you down. You accumulate all these *nouns* in your life. Persons, places, things you love. There are *years* of nouns around you when you're a middle-aged divorced grieving mother. And most of my nouns were gone. All I had left was *me*. I had my daughter and my family and my old cat. I had my memories and my dreams, and sometimes the two were the same.

But I wouldn't believe all my dreams were in the past. I *believed* my own mantra, and I was already making some of it happen. I had a job and I was moving to Colorado, all expenses paid. I now realized I had been placing obstacles in front of myself, instead of seeing past them. And once you achieve a level of success in manifesting beyond those obstacles, you become much more focused on achieving *all* your dreams. I was becoming very deliberate in my own creation of the life I still dreamed of.

Terryee knew what a rough day I was having, and she called me several times while I was driving to Denver in a snow storm. She always gets you up when you're down. She gets you focused on achieving the abundance you desire, rather than letting you wallow in your own misery. And Terryee makes you *believe* you can.

Three months later, I signed with a publisher. Eleven months after I moved, I had a copy of my own book in my hands for Christmas. Does manifesting work? I'm living near my daughter in Colorado, and you're reading my published work.

I've used manifesting techniques to draw people, situations, and achievements into my life. My friend, Greg Ryan, told me he started asking God to bring people into his life who *he* can help, instead of asking for people who can help *him*. Confident in the law of karma, Greg knew if he helped other people, the favors would be returned. He began seeing amazing results. I started doing the same thing and I was astounded at how many people suddenly showed up asking for my assistance with something, and those people had connections or knowledge which enabled me to succeed at something *I* was manifesting for. Ask God to bring people to you who need *your* help, and trust that you will get the help you desire from others.

Greg is a success story unto himself. He left his home with a box that contained $200 and set off for California when he was in his early twenties. He had a degree in Architecture and he competed in body building competitions. Greg quickly landed a job at a fitness studio and soon became a fitness guru for the celebrities. He had started with $200 and a belief in his own success. Greg has reinvented himself countless times since then, and excelled at everything he set his sights on. Architectural design, abstract art, musical performance, personal training, authoring numerous books on fitness and spiritual motivation, and management of a country music group. I should mention, Greg has ADHD and sensory integration autism. He's a living example of someone who sees past the obstacles and shoots for his dreams, no excuses.

Greg is a huge inspiration to me, and he motivates everyone he comes into contact with. You can reach Greg at gregryanfitness@yahoo.com.

When I first met Greg socially, I liked him immediately, but I would have never guessed he had any sort of a learning disability. After I heard his story, I felt nudged to work with him. Because of my son's autism, I knew Greg could be a huge inspiration to others with any form of autism or ADHD, as well as their families. My introduction to Greg seemed to be one of those serendipitous moments that I believe to be instigated by a higher being. I don't believe in coincidences. Everyone is brought into your life for a reason. Sometimes those reasons are obvious, and sometimes you only realize them later.

When you are deliberately creating the career or the life you want, you'll be amazed at the people who pop into your life unexpectedly and seem to pull you up in the direction you need to go. Greg did that for me. When he was bidding adieu to one of his elderly clients in Kentucky, she asked him why he was moving his business to Colorado. He told her, "I just feel like that's where I need to be right now. I know there's someone I can help out there. I just haven't met them yet."

I know I'm not the only person in Colorado whose life has been impacted by Greg, but I'm happy to count myself as one who he has helped and inspired. Plus, he's really hot.

Soul Agreements

Terryee is inundated with phone calls from people asking when they are going to meet their soul mate. Do we have only one soul mate? It would seem awfully hard to meet that perfect partner if there was only one. When we're in love with someone, we can't imagine falling in love with someone else, and we verbalize that feeling often. And then years down the road, we do fall in love with someone else, and we look back and wonder how we could have believed the previous person was our only "ideal" mate. So what exactly is a soul mate? Is there only one person who would be our perfect partner for a lifetime? If we met this perfect mate at a young age, would we stay madly in love with them until the day we die?

Soul mates are people who we have made soul agreements with. We have agreed to show up for each other in this life in a relationship of some particular form. It may be in a romantic form, it might be a familial form, or simply a friendship form of relationship.

Before we talk about soul agreements, we first need to present the idea of pre-determined lessons. The idea of reincarnation is not easily embraced, even by us. Who wants to come back here for more painful lessons? We like the idea of leaving the harsh realities of earth life behind and never looking back. Does this make sense?

Here are some points to consider. Is life fair? No. Would a fair God randomly choose some souls to enter a comfortable life full of love, and some souls begin life with two strikes against them? Why did those souls draw the short straws? Were they *bad*? Would God create anything that wasn't perfect? Did that newborn baby with heart defects come into the world with more original sin than the rest of us?

Why do some people struggle with taking ownership, while others struggle to let go of control? How did God decide which souls will merit more opportunities for prosperity? Or who is born with physical beauty and who is not?

We believe in a fair God. We also believe God is continually working with all of us, as a mentor, as we go through each life lesson. And yes, we believe God is the final judge and jury, but He is also the kindest, most compassionate father in the universe. He realizes his children screw up, and He is always ready and waiting at the finish line with a box of Kleenex and words of wisdom. He's here to teach us, and He has an army of angels and archangels to help us, just as a school superintendent has an army of teachers and principals.

If it's difficult to entertain the idea of coming back here for different life lessons, then also consider our belief that it's *your* choice to come back or not. Feel better? We don't believe God forces us to reincarnate, but rather, He encourages us to keep evolving our souls in ways that we *agree* upon. Ultimately, many of us decide it will benefit us to re-enter this physical existence with a different set of circumstances to work through than we had in a previous life. But we're never alone in the classroom. We have angels and guides and God at our shoulder, urging us to make good decisions. We also have our classmates who have incarnated with us, in differing roles. Unlike school, however, there is no predetermined length of time before you're allowed to graduate. If it takes you longer than four years to master all the material between freshman and senior status, that's okay. Some of us have many lifetimes of 'sophomore year' before we learn all the lessons required for ascension to a higher level of being.

Before entering life, we have studied ourselves in depth – with a lot of heavenly guidance, and clearly outlined the issues we need to work on the most. We agree on a set of circumstances for our next life which will allow us the opportunity to do the most effective work on those issues. In other words, we *choose* the life we are born into. We choose some of the defining moments of that life, but we also understand we will have free will to make decisions during those moments. Contradictory to the saying, "You can't choose your family;" your family is one of the essential choices you make.

While that idea may be hard to swallow, consider your own family. You have learned extremely important lessons from them, whether through *good* example or *bad* example. The form of the example doesn't matter, but only the fact that you learned the important lesson. Your life lessons are not about *them*. Your life is about *you*. It's like learning to ride a bike. Some people believe the training wheels should be left on until the rider has attained a high degree of balance. And some swear they quickly learned how to ride a bike because they had *no* training wheels, and they learned to conquer their fear out of necessity instead of harmless repetition. There are many people who feel they learn best through trial by fire, while most feel more comfortable easing into things gradually. Neither method is right or wrong. The only thing that's important is that everyone will learn how to ride a bike.

Certain situations in your life will be pivotal. Most of those milestone moments have been predetermined. Some of those moments are happy times, and some are terribly painful. But when the world comes crashing down on you, it causes you to stop in your tracks and take a different path with a different outlook and a different set of priorities. Invariably, the new priorities are more heart-based.

How many people have told you the most awful occurrence in their life turned out to be the best thing that could have happened to them, spiritually? How many stories have we heard of an athlete, cut down in his prime with a physical injury, who lives to tell the story of the life-changing event that ultimately made him a better person?

Looking back on your life, hasn't there been an unwelcome event that you now realize created positive change in you? But at the time, you couldn't imagine anything positive would result. Those types of events were predetermined or fated, and they were meant to teach you important life lessons. You chose them, although you currently have no recollection of making that choice.

If you are stuck in a victim mentality, this ideology will not make sense to you, and you will quickly dismiss it as "new age garbage." But if you are a person who enjoys taking ownership of their life, it may begin to resonate with you and perhaps, make sense.

> Johnny grew up in a rural farming community where he was a big fish in a little pond. He inherited his mother's striking good looks and his father's charm. His parents were highly regarded in the community for their benevolence toward those less fortunate. They were not rich by any means, but they were always the first to come to the aid of a fellow neighbor when disaster struck, and they gave away as much hay as they sold. A chiseled physique was the only advantage Johnny saw to laboring in the fields for hours helping his dad. He secretly believed the beneficiaries of

his father's good will should be helping him stack the hay bales in the sweltering heat. But through his toil, he enabled himself to catch the attention of the athletic coaches, who noted Johnny's immense strength. Johnny became a star athlete in high school, which gave him the opportunity to advance himself with a scholarship. Leaving the farm and his family behind, Johnny left for greener pastures and never looked back. Years later, he had acquired all the trappings of a successful yuppie, including a Harley. By his own account, he felt extremely proud of the 'stuff' he had obtained, but not so proud of himself. The more he accumulated, the more his self-worth suffered. Johnny would remember his father spending hours working on the old pick-up he had driven for years, coaxing its engine to life one more time, since buying a new vehicle was not an affordable option. But his dad would get that pick-up fired up if someone had livestock starving for food which the owner couldn't afford to buy. And off he would go to deliver the hay that Johnny had loaded for him, with the engine wheezing and coughing over the dirt roads.

Johnny was not without a heart, and he regularly gave back to his parents. They always told him he shouldn't waste his hard-earned money on them, and he always told them he wanted them to have nice things; to which they always assured him they had the nicest thing God could have given them: Johnny.

Johnny's pivotal moment occurred during a peaceful ride through the foothills near Denver. He frequently rode his Harley up to his favorite mountain-top bar on the weekends when the weather was nice. He enjoyed taking the scenic back roads, and didn't feel it necessary to don a helmet when he wasn't going to be cruising at highway speeds. On this particular evening, it started to rain. He considered pulling over and waiting out the rain, but visibility was still good and he knew he'd make it home in twenty minutes.

One slippery curve on that short ride home resulted in permanent paralysis from the waist down, and limited mobility in his torso from the neck down. Johnny's life was forever changed. I met Johnny when he enlisted my assistance at a store that I managed.

After thanking me for pulling down an item that he could not reach from his wheelchair, Johnny remarked, "You've got a smile that comes from the *inside*."

"Thank you! It does, believe it or not. Even when the outside looks pissed," I joked. "I can say the same about you, but your smile actually resonates from your eyes. I see peace there."

"There *is*." Johnny stated firmly. "But I had to go to hell and back to find it. And by going to hell, I don't mean getting paralyzed. My motorcycle accident was a huge wake-up call for me. The hell I went through was in the realization that I had been ashamed of who I was and where I came from."

Johnny shared his story with me. "I was never ashamed of my parents, but I always thought I was so much *smarter* than they were. I always told myself I was never going to get taken advantage of, the way I saw people take advantage of my dad's kind heart. I was never going to have to struggle for money. It was always going to be *me* first, then my parents, and then no one. I never had compassion for anyone that hadn't done something for me first. I would pay *back*, but I would never just *give*. And then I found myself flat on my back and depending on the compassion of everyone around me. Strangers. People who didn't *owe* me anything. And it's amazing to see the kindness of strangers. And then my parents."

Johnny's voiced cracked, and he paused to compose himself. "I will never forgive myself for causing the pain I saw in their eyes when they saw me in the hospital. Their prodigal son. The hometown hero. Some hero!" he laughed. "They had to wipe my ass for me, once again, and painfully watch as I had to learn how to feed myself, dress myself, everything all over again. I swear there are not any two people on earth who can love as much as those two people love me."

Then a twinkle returned to Johnny's eyes as he resumed, "I learned what love really means at age thirty-four....from my parents.....who had tried to show me all my life, but I was too self-absorbed to get it. And now at age thirty-seven I'm trying to *show* it. Fell in love with one of my therapists and we're getting married in a couple of months. I took up jewelry making as part of my rehab, and I'm making her a wedding ring myself. I made my dad a watch with an old pick-up etched into the face. I don't think he's ever felt prouder of anything I've given him, including the sports trophies. I'm trying to figure out how to make a wedding band with a heart that has a Harley emblem hidden in it. I never would have met my soul mate if I hadn't taken that ride. It was the best thing that ever happened to me. It sounds weird, but I really feel like it was meant to happen. The whole thing: The accident; meeting Lori; re-establishing a closer relationship with my parents. I swear it was fate. I will never believe my accident was an accident."

I shared my favorite quotation with Johnny. I wish I knew who to credit this quote to, but it was shared with me by a friend after I lost my son.

"My friend told me, 'Nothing bad ever happens. There are just different versions of sweet and sour.' Like me, you choose to savor the sweet."

Johnny's story is a poignant illustration of someone who can view his life from an objective standpoint. He didn't get caught up in the victim stance of asking, "Why me?" He could easily see a higher purpose in his apparent misfortune. This is the brand of thinking we are trying to impart in this book. Stop feeling like you are the victim of life, and start owning your life experiences. You chose them for a reason.

Terryee struggled with self-esteem and self-worth issues much of her life. The gift of clairvoyance can easily feel like a curse when you are young and trying to fit in with your peers. She never liked her body. Terryee loved ballet and she wanted the asexual figure that was customary on the prima ballerinas, and loathed her ample bust line. She was never overweight, but she viewed herself as chubby in comparison to other dancers. If she could have whacked her own boobs off, she would have.

The issues she'd had with her body image came as a surprise to me. Terryee looks like the petite blonde Barbie doll that every young girl aspires to be. She's gorgeous and glowing with healthy skin washed by the sun, and her clear blue eyes have the color and depth of the ocean she lives by. Years of dancing have given her long legs a beautiful tone, and her hands have the expressive elegance of a ballerina. Even her feet are pretty. Being a former shoe store manager, I've seen plenty of ugly feet in my time, and had firmly concluded that all feet are ugly. And then I met Terryee, who bounced into my life with her pedicured toenails flashing across perfect little tanned feet; a beautiful bundle of energy, compassion, and wisdom. And sassiness. I loved her immediately; she felt like a soul sister.

Terryee had suffered through numerous complications with her diabetes. She had been hospitalized at age ten, and she had spent years undergoing the constant changes with her insulin dosage, which was ever-increasing.

By the summer of 2010, Terryee was feeling tired, lethargic, and overwhelmed. She took a trip to visit her father, and contracted the swine flu when she was down there. Within days, Terryee was hospitalized with diabetic complications, barely able to speak in a rasp, and her organs were shutting down. Her greatest diabetic fear appeared to be coming true, as blindness started creeping in and darkening everything around her.

But her psychic vision was crystal clear. While lying in the hospital, Terryee saw three big angels who came to speak to her. Terryee has been seeing angels and spirits since she was a child, so this did not come as an unwanted surprise to her. The angels were accompanied by Jesus.

The angels told her, "You will heal yourself of diabetes."

Terryee whispered with her usual humor, "Why don't *you* heal me? You're angels and I'm dying here."

"You're not going to die," they assured her. "You are a healer and you're going to heal yourself."

This started her journey of becoming a light healer. She'd always known she had the ability to heal, but she had not tested herself or proven it to others. Terryee believes she chose diabetes as a way of forcing herself to prove to *herself* that she is a healer.

She began working with a nutritional expert and performing reiki on herself. Terryee began to closely monitor everything she was putting into her body. She started exercising again, as her strength gradually came back and her vision improved. Within months, she had reduced her insulin usage dramatically.

Several epiphanies came to Terryee while in her degenerated state. She had always struggled with self-worth and self-love issues. She had never learned to love her own body, and she knew she constantly struggled with issues from previous lives. Her own family had been different participants in previous lives they had shared together, and she remembered being the brunt of cruel teasing about her weight during the last life. It affected her and demoralized her in the current life experience, and she finally started confronting her own demons.

For years, Terryee had been helping other people, while neglecting her own self-love issues. Armed with a smile and a wisecrack, she threw herself into her work and tried to keep shutting the closet door on the issues that kept spilling out when she least expected. That's what we do with old emotional baggage. We hurry and close the door on it so we don't have to look at it, but it always comes seeping out behind our back. Until you confront your own issues, you will continually be reminded of the mess you're hiding in your closet.

Terryee finally understood self-worth on a personal level. As she remarks, "It only matters what *I* think of me! It doesn't matter what anyone else thinks. It's not about them, it's about me. My journey with diabetes was all about healing myself, and believing in myself and my own ability as a healer. But it had to start inside of me first. I had to love myself, love my body, and love my spirit as much as I love my creator. It's about seeing yourself as an extension of God. We are all God in some way. He works through us to heal ourselves and others. When we give love to ourselves, we are loving God. We're valuing the qualities of God that are inside of us, and we're sharing them with others. I know I chose diabetes to bring that realization to myself in this life. I'm healing the old karma, and I'm balanced now."

It may be difficult to imagine yourself choosing health issues, money problems, career crises, or romantic heartbreak for yourself, but the wisdom acquired from pain and suffering evolves our souls, which is the reason we're here. It's your choice to make sweet or sour lemonade. You can choose to become bitter and angry and self-pitying, and the growth potential will be wasted. That's where free will steps in. It's your choice to do what you want with your pain. Use it or lose it.

Soul Mates

Groups of souls reincarnate together as a soul family. They are not necessarily family members in this life. They may be friends, lovers, spouses, colleagues or relatives. They travel through lifetimes together, helping each other as they are all working on their own lessons. Their lives may be intricately woven together or they may come together for a brief time to work on a short lesson. Usually both souls will benefit in some way, although sometimes it appears that one soul just popped in to teach the other soul a quick lesson, or give them a boost of support. Even in those instances, the soul who is teaching is still a beneficiary. They are imparting a lesson that was given to them by someone else, and it's the karmic version of paying it forward. Or they could be coming back to balance the karma with the soul they are showing up to help. In a karmic sense, there are no bad guys, so we hate to use the phrase, "settling a debt," but that's sort of the idea of karmic balance. We have all hurt others, and we have all been hurt ourselves. We have all been guilty of lying, cheating, betraying, stealing, and demoralizing others; if not in this life, then in previous lives. We have also loved, forgiven, supported, and nurtured. We are all both yin and yang.

Souls agree to play certain roles in each other's lives for the purpose of learning and growing. While the reason behind the relationship is supported by love, the relationship may not always feel loving. In fact, some souls who are supporting our growth are doing so in the form of a nemesis. They may be an enemy in the current life. They could be a scornful parent, an unloving spouse, or an archrival at work. They have agreed to play the 'bad guy' in your life to help you learn to stand up for yourself, or find your own value, or learn to truly forgive. They may have agreed to play the example for others in how *not* to be. Some people say the only thing they learned from their parents was how *not* to be a good parent. But they did become good parents themselves, so apparently their bad parents played their roles well. We're not excusing those 'bad' parents for not exercising free will and choosing to become better parents. They were given a choice, too. But essentially, the roles were set up prior to birth, and both parties accepted the terms, which included the worst case scenario.

The modern day use of the term "soul mate" is usually describing a romantic relationship, but soul mates are simply two souls who came into this life with an agreement to show up for each other in some capacity. They might be best friends, father and son, husband and wife, and so on. You may have many soul mates in your life time. We are discussing three different types of soul mate relationships: karmic soul mates, companion soul mates, and twin soul/twin flame soul mates. Different people have very differing philosophies on soul mates. Some believe there is only one person who will *feel* like the other half of you, when you meet them. Others believe that the soul has actually split itself before entering life, and the soul mate *is* the other half of the soul. In essence, that would be a reverse image of two people in one; but one soul in two bodies instead. While we don't discount anything, including parallel lives, we will stick with the familiar idea of separate souls.

Karmic Soul Mates

This relationship is usually the most painful. Two souls are coming together to resolve karma from a previous life or previous relationship. It's essentially payback time for one or both of them. You're balancing karma in this type of soul mate relationship. There is usually an undeniably strong attraction with a karmic soul mate. It may be a parent/child relationship, friends, lovers, or family. You feel magnetically bonded to that person. If it's a romantic relationship, the passion will usually heat up quickly. You may believe this lover is your twin flame, or the other half of your soul. Difficult and painful lessons are learned through karmic relationships, but once the karma is balanced, the final lesson is all about learning to let go. With family or lifelong relationships, it may be an ongoing struggle until one of them dies. With romantic relationships, they usually end painfully, sometimes abruptly, as soon as the karma between them is balanced. Karmic soul mates feel like a 'have to', rather than a 'want to.' You don't know why, but you feel inexplicably drawn to that relationship, even if there are warning bells ringing. It's a soul obligation, although relating to that person probably won't initially feel like a duty, but rather a desire. The universe will supply you with all the right signals to enter into that relationship. If it is a family member, such as your mother, you will continue to see situations arise that demand your participation in that relationship. In many instances it's a spouse or a love interest. You may start feeling like the relationship is poison, but you have a very difficult time leaving it. You will not be able to extricate yourself from a karmic relationship until you've balanced the karma between yourself and that individual. Even then, it's very difficult to leave a relationship that's still loaded with heavy emotional baggage. Then it becomes a test for you to show *yourself* love by leaving it behind. Abusive relationships can be like this.

> Sophia was an engineer at an aerospace company, and she married Phillip, who was a wealthy real estate investor. Phillip enjoyed pampering Sophia and taking care of all the household duties, and she was happy to turn over a lot of responsibilities to him. He seemed to enjoy having control over the household, and she was thankful she had less on her plate to worry about. Sophia enjoyed the attention he lavished upon her when she got home, and he frequently offered to pamper her by giving her a bath. Phillip gradually started controlling

more and more details of her life, and she began feeling uncomfortable when he practically insisted on bathing her himself. He became emotionally and verbally abusive if she did not succumb to his wishes. Sophia called Terryee for some guidance.

"Have you ever had a past life regression?" Terryee inquired. "I see there's some karma you're bringing in here with Phillip. He wants to control you, and there's something going on with that. You are the one in control of the situation, though. It's your choice to leave or stay with him, but things are not going to get better. He wants to control every area of your life. He won't leave *you*, though. You actually have all the control here."

Sophia said she'd give it some thought, and called Terryee back several months later to report, "I had been having strange flashbacks at times, and I did not understand what they were. I finally did as you suggested, and I started piecing together the flashbacks I was having. Phillip was my father in a previous life. I trusted him and he sexually abused me. The bathing thing tied into that. I was meant to unite with again, and leave him this time. He owed me.

"Part of my karmic balance was the act of forgiving myself. I had done nothing wrong to him in our previous life, and I had suffered through his abuse. I felt like a prisoner, and I needed to come back and free myself this time. I'm not a prisoner. I'm not broken and I don't need fixed. He was repeating the abusive behavior to give me a chance to free myself this time, since I was unable to do so as a child. I needed to forgive him, but mostly, I needed to forgive myself for the guilt I had felt. I needed to find that balance."

In this situation, the karmic "debt" was settled in this life, and Sophia and Phillip could reincarnate together again and have a healthy relationship without any bad karma between them. No one is an enemy on the other side. No grudges are carried over there, but the "debt" will be settled over *here*, and the karma will be balanced. And yes, for some, karma is a bitch.

But just think of how much the mean people must love us on the other side. They agreed to be the bad guys in our life in order for us to learn a valuable lesson. Who wants to be the bad guy, for the primary purpose of being someone else's teacher? Are they learning anything except how deep-down shitty you feel when you hurt people? Maybe that was *their* lesson.

Think of unresolved karma as a balancing act on the scales of justice. If you're not familiar with dish scales, then think of it as a teeter-totter. You and I were incarnated in the last life as equals; we both put equal weight on our ends of the teeter-totter, so we were both suspended at an equal height. I got selfish, and I decided to throw fifty pounds of pain onto your lap. Your side of the teeter-totter became weighted down with misery, while I was flying high on my end, acting like an asshole. Our lives ended, and we both moved over into the spirit world, where we all lose our tarnish from earthly lives. We're reborn into our authentic loving selves, and we don't have the earthly motivation for selfishness. I see the error of my ways, and you are no longer holding a grudge. We don't have self-worth issues of the ego, and we all realize ourselves as equal children of God. In the other dimension, I feel badly for hurting you, and I want to be fair and equitable. You forgive me, but universal fairness dictates a balance of power. So I agree to reincarnate with you and allow you to balance the karma. This time around, you get to throw fifty pounds of pain onto *my* lap, and suddenly our teeter-totter seats are even again. We're balanced. We won't carry the old karma with us into the next life time, unless one of us decides to exercise our free will and jack up the karma again. I sure hope you don't act like a bigger asshole than I did. I like you. But if you do, there's always a next time. Just remember, karma really can be a bitch when she's menopausal. Just sayin'.

Twin Flame Soul Mates

These are often described as twin souls. They are as if you have mirrored yourself in another form, male or female. Twin flames are not presented to us in every lifetime, as they require a higher level of ascension to participate in a twin soul relationship. It does not necessarily mean it's a romantic relationship. Well known psychic Edgar Cayce believed a twin flame relationship was a shared mental connection, while companion souls shared a spiritual connection. He believed his wife was a soul mate, while his secretary was his twin flame. We believe in the common assumption that a twin flame can be both working partner *and* lover, and perhaps this is what makes that relationship so difficult for some. Both partners are coming together to work on something that's important to both of them in this lifetime together. Romantic twin flames have the added weight of their love relationship to maneuver alongside the other work they're doing together. It may be working side by side in an office, in the arts, or doing charity work together. There is usually some kind of forum or idea outside the relationship that both partners are passionate about pursuing. Twin soul love connections are never easy, and both partners need to be ready before they are presented with that kind of a relationship. It requires the strength of evolved souls who have loved and lost over many lifetimes. It's not for the weak or faint hearted. Love is not a bed of roses with a twin flame, and it requires the ability to love and forgive unconditionally. It's like loving yourself, with all of your faults exposed. It may require loving and letting go of a partner who feels more comfortable with a less intense soul mate relationship, where they feel less vulnerable. It does not guarantee a happy ending, but it's a true test of one's ability to love without the condition of receiving anything in return. The ultimate unity is in one's own soul. To truly experience love, we need to feel whole and complete unto ourselves. Loving a soul mate is a shared extension of that love, which comes from God.

> Paula and Jacob met on the job in their early thirties and felt an immediate kinship, but Jacob was married. They worked side by side together every day at the advertising agency, and felt completely in sync with each other. They shared responsibility for writing promotional material for area businesses. Many private jokes were exchanged between them, stemming from their difficulty in dreaming up catchy slogans to drum up business for hospitals. A flirtation began, and soon they had fallen madly in love. Jacob was still married to his wife, and they had small children. Paula decided it was futile and selfish of her to split up a family with small children, so she broke it off with Jacob and left her job. Jacob made a habit of reaching out to her every once in a while, but Paula tried to move on with her life, dating other men.

> Paula contacted Terryee one day and asked the first half of the M & M question, "Do you see any men coming into my life soon?"

> Terryee thought for a moment. "I see a man who you have a heart connection with. You're separated from him now. But the heart connection is still there. He's married? I see a

female energy around him, but there's no love connection. I do see they have children, though."

"Yes," Paula sighed. "I fell madly in love with Jacob, and I left my job in order to leave him. I could not allow myself to split up a family. It was wrong."

"I respect you for that," Terryee assured her. "But I do see the two of you reconnecting at some point."

"I would be the happiest woman alive. But I don't think the situation will change. I keep trying to move on and meet someone else, but I just haven't met anyone I care about. I don't want to keep my life on hold, but I keep thinking about Jacob."

"I agree that you need to keep moving forward, and dating other men. And as a woman, I want to tell you to forget him since he's married with kids. But as a psychic, I can't tell you that it's over with him. You're twin souls. You're moving about, doing different things and living different lives, but there's still a very strong connection between you, even if you're not interacting with each other. But you're right. Don't live your life in a pause moment. Keep going out and living your life, but don't mentally close the door on anything or anyone."

Seven years later, a divorced Jacob asked Paula to marry him. He had spent the last seven years building his own advertising agency, and he wanted Paula to join him as a partner. Jacob had built the business for them to be able to work together, once again.

Paula now laughs, as she tells her story. "I was absolutely miserable without him, but I convinced myself I was going to get over him and meet the soul mate that I trusted God would bring me. And God didn't let me down."

Companion Soul Mates

This is the easiest relationship by far. Once again, these soul mates can take any form of relationship, and they are probably the easiest for marriage. Companion souls feel like a comfortable old pair of jeans. They're easy to be with and the drama is usually minimal. These are soul mates you are not bringing in a lot of difficult karma with. They have agreed to walk hand in hand with you during your journey together, and you agreed to support each other. It's like a best friend. You feel a strong loving bond between you. Companion soul mates who marry each other can also feel a very strong physical bond and attraction. Great sex is not limited to karmic soul mates and twin flames!

So what if two souls have a pre-life agreement and one of them exercises free will and decides to take a different path? Does this happen? Yes. People are always presented with different choices, and that is part of the learning experience. Not every person will take the direction their heart or their conscience is telling them to take. Their brain may be sending them different signals. Their fear may drive them down a different road. If this happens, all is not lost. The universe will see to it that another soul is brought in to replace the soul that opted out of the agreement. As in retail, the substitute soul mate will be of equal or greater value! So don't despair if your soul mate decides to take a different course. Trust in the abundant universe and let them go. Letting go will allow a new partner to come in and fill the void. If you try to hang on to the partner that walked away, you will push the arrival of another partner away from you. Learning to let go is key when you're talking about soul mates. Unconditional love means loving yourself first, and feeling complete and whole when you are alone. When you struggle to feel like a "whole" person without your partner, then you need to ask yourself where that feeling is coming from. Why do you feel lacking? When you truly love someone as the angels love, you long for that person when they're not with you, but you're not dependent on them to make you feel worthy and lovable. You ache for their presence, but your own value is not diminished in your own eyes if they are not beside you.

Lastly, there are souls who enter this life primarily to learn how to stand on their own. They will have loving relationships from members of their soul family, but they are not searching for that "one and only" soul mate. These people are quite normal, and they don't need any fixer-ups. They're learning the lessons they're meant to learn in this lifetime, and they're quite happy without a partner. If you have single friends who profess to be happier alone, believe them. They are enjoying their own experience.

We all need to learn how to feel whole and complete without a partner. Most of us desperately long for that great love of our life, but the biggest lesson we need to learn is that we don't need a significant other to feel whole unto ourselves. We're worthy alone, as individuals. We don't need the status of a mate, or the security it brings our pathetic little egos who don't want to be alone.

If you share real, unconditional love with another being, that is the most wonderful experience in the world. But if you're just looking for a companion or a paycheck to save you from standing on your own, then you're not looking for real, unconditional love. You're looking for a sugar-daddy or a mother figure. You don't want to be by yourself because you don't like your own company. You should know better than us. Are you that annoying to be around?

Especially For Women

Listen up, girlfriends. What is the first thing you always think of when meeting a new man? *I hope he likes me.* This is *not* what you should be thinking. You should be wondering, *Will I like him? Does he represent what I want in a partner?* This is all about you, not him. Right at this minute, do you think he is wondering if you'll like him? No, he's thinking about the tires on his car or the conversation he had with his boss today. He's wondering if you'll like fishing, but it doesn't bother him if you don't. He's still got his friends to go with him.

Men have the ability to compartmentalize everything in their lives, while women connect everything. Men can have an argument with their spouse and go to work and forget about it, while it will ruin their spouse's day. Terryee and I are envious of the way men can do this. It's like certain parts of their brains operate separately, at different times. Our brains are wired differently, with everything interconnected in the same household. If one fuse blows, the lights go out in the entire house.

A lot of men we know can happily date someone who only has a few qualities they find endearing and attractive. It's almost as if they have compartmentalized the woman herself. She's

99

beautiful. Check. She likes my friends. Check. We're good to go.

Meanwhile, there are a million little things they don't find attractive about the woman. She's not too sharp. She has a grating voice. She has no interest in anything the man likes to do. She can't hold a job. Her family is annoying and interfering. She's not dependable. The list of cons might go on forever, and yet the man seems blissfully happy with his relationship. It's not that he's unaware of the negatives, but he doesn't focus on them and stew about them all day like we do.

Women need to have everything firing on all four cylinders in their lives. So if there's a problem with their most important relationship, their whole world is affected. This is why it's important to enter a new relationship with a clear idea of what you desire in a partner. If you're tired of false starts with dead end relationships, then it would behoove you to actually make of list of attributes you wish your partner to have. Make a list of all the qualities you desire in a partner, and you can't be too specific. Describe the ways in which you want your partner to demonstrate those qualities.

For example, if *thoughtful* is a quality on your list, then elaborate on what this means to you. "He remembers my work schedule and doesn't need to be reminded of when I'm not available." Or, "He leaves the toilet seat down." Or, "He sneaks greeting cards into my suitcase." Whatever your version of *thoughtful* is, write down some examples.

How about *loyal*? We all want loyalty. But what does that mean to you? Does it mean he never sleeps around, but it's okay if he flirts with other women? Or does it mean he defends you to your sister if she chastises your cooking? Does it mean he continually reassures you of his fidelity and undying love for you? Or does it mean he reassures you on an hourly basis, and he never appears to even notice the beauty of other women? Be clear on what your words mean to you.

I've learned the hard way, be careful what you ask for. After struggling through multiple relationships with men who were afraid of commitment, I said I wanted a man with 'no fear.' Terryee kept telling me I needed to get clear on what I wanted, and I thought I was being clear by asking for a man with no fear. I got one. My next boyfriend was a very tough and very muscular 'man's man,' with no tolerance for weakness or emotional tenderness. No tenderness at all, not even in the bedroom. I had to remind myself that I asked for that, as I limped away from his bed every morning. No fear. Check. Advil. Che.....where the hell's the Advil?

So be clear on the qualities you want, and how they are represented in your ideal partner. The importance of actually writing a list is that it gives you clarity on what you're looking for. Reading it frequently will keep it fresh in your mind, and you'll find you can more easily walk away from someone who doesn't represent that list well – before your heart strings grow attached to that person.

Terryee calls her most frequently asked questions, "The M & M questions." Men and money.

> "When am I going to meet the man of my dreams?"

> "When is he going to call me?"

> "Why doesn't he say he loves me?"

Women wish they could get inside of a man's brain and discover what he's thinking. We often assume he's thinking about another woman or a reason to leave us. That's our fear talking. A man will take our relationship out of its compartment and look at it when it's right in front of his face. But he's not constantly analyzing it the way we do. He takes it out and looks it over, and then puts it back in its compartment.

Terryee has done thousands of readings for male clients, and she's rarely met a man who doesn't have that ability to compartmentalize. They can separate areas of their life and think about each thing in its own realm, while women are more compulsive and we want everything smoothly meshed together. We want immediate results, immediate feedback, and immediate connectedness. If something feels wrong about the relationship, we want it resolved right now. We can't put it aside and get back to it later.

Richard is in love with Bonnie, and convinced she's the right partner for him, but she wasn't giving him enough of her time and attention. So Richard decided to just let her go and move onto other things. He simply threw himself into his job and put the relationship aside, mentally. He stopped calling Bonnie and it appeared that she was "out of sight, out of mind."

Suddenly, Bonnie started calling *him*. She was assuming he had gotten over her and moved on to be with another woman. Bonnie assumed Richard's withdrawal meant he no longer loved her. But Richard was still very much in love with her; he just didn't feel the compulsion to try to connect with someone who pushed him away. He could put the relationship on a shelf and concentrate on other things.

Ladies, you need to understand that it doesn't mean a man doesn't love you, just because he isn't thinking about the relationship all the time, and beating your door down.

If you don't have that man of your dreams, how do you attract him? Nothing says "sexy" like a self-confident woman, so you better go back to the earlier chapter and start working on your own self-worth issues. You don't need to be beautiful to be self-assured. A self-confident woman *is* beautiful to men. Secondly, you need to have your own life going on. Men are attracted to women who don't *need* them.

Men are hunters. They love the hunt; the thrill of the chase. Men need to reach for us. They're attracted to women they have to work to connect with. Don't be clingy and insecure and needy. And don't give everything away. Men love a little mystery. They like wondering what the woman is doing. While women love certainty, men like a little *un*certainty. And they like watching us squirm. If they know their behavior is making us wonder about them, they'll often continue that behavior, knowing we're thinking about them all the time.

> Michael is successful, independent, and good looking. His relationship with Roxanne has lasted longer than any of his other romances because he has to stretch for her. He does most of the work. Roxanne is successful, independent, self-reliant, and busy with her own life. She's the only woman who has maintained Michael's attention, simply because he has a hard time getting hers.

This may sounds sophomoric to a lot of women, but the truth is that no matter how old they are, men are still attracted to the one that's hard to get. Their hunter instincts rise to the surface, and their ego directs them to pursue. While they may want to marry a woman who nurtures them like their mother did, a nurturing single woman may not find herself with many dates if she appears to be an easy conquest.

Men like you to be their best friend. They like to bounce things off you and enjoy the camaraderie they feel with their other male buddies. So don't ignore him when he's talking about that amazing play he made in the softball tournament, or the headaches he has at the office. Many friendships have turned into romances. But lots of romances have fizzled when the friendship was no longer being fostered. Men like you to listen to them as much as you want them to listen to you.

> Frank and Cindy met at work. Frank was taking care of his elderly mother, whose health was failing. Cindy developed a crush on Frank and his face always lit up when he saw her, but he hadn't asked her out.

> Cindy called Terryee, asking for guidance. "I really like this guy at work. I think he likes me too. I mean, he seems to *like* me a lot, but he's never asked me out. We have lunch together and we talk about everything and anything, and we laugh all the time. I can tell he's always really happy to see me, but he's never said anything that slightly hinted at developing a romantic relationship outside of the office. Do you think he has any feelings for me that way?"

> Terryee thought for a moment. "Yes, I see that he does, but he's burdened down with something. Is it his mother? I can see he's taking care of an older woman. I'm sure it's his mom."

105

"Yes," Cindy replied. "He talks to me about his mom all the time. She's dying and it's been really hard on him. His sister lives in another state so all the care-taking of their mom has landed solely on Frank's shoulders. That's one of the things I love about him. He never complains about the work and stress involved, but he's going through a rough time watching his mother die. He feels guilty if he's at work and she's alone, and then he feels guilty when he has to run out the door at five o'clock everyday if other people are working late."

"Yeah, I think he's a really good guy," Terryee assured her. "He's just feeling overwhelmed right now. He's put dating on the back burner. There's a real easy chemistry there between you two, and he loves it as much as you do. You just need to hang in there. He's going to ask you out. He's so weighted down right now; he wouldn't notice it if a naked woman was jumping on his desk. Just be his friend now."

Cindy followed Terryee's advice and continued being a friend to Frank, and they're now happily engaged. Frank says he loved the fact that he could talk to Cindy about work, his mom, and his frustrations. She didn't make him feel pressured during a time when he had enormous pressure in other areas of his life. Cindy was his friend, and is now his fiancée.

In order get that man of your dreams, you have to make yourself available to them. Perhaps that seems elementary to you, but apparently everyone doesn't see it that way.

"When is my soul mate going to come to me?" the caller asked Terryee.

"I can see you sitting in your house a lot," Terryee observed. "Do you ever get out?"

"No, not really," Ruth replied.

"Do you go to church groups or social functions where you meet men?" Terryee asked.

"No, I don't like groups," Ruth replied.

Terryee tried to guide Ruth, without slapping her in the face with the obvious truth of what she "saw" in Ruth's future. "How 'bout the grocery store? You ever get out and talk to people when you go shopping?"

"No." Ruth was getting agitated.

"Well, tell me, Ruth," Terryee asked, "Have you ever thought of trying to meet a man on a dating web site?"

"No! I don't want to meet another man! I want my soul mate! I'm sitting right here waiting for him to come find me!" Ruth snapped.

True story.

The Men's Turn

What do women want? Certainty. Don't over-promise and under-deliver in relationships with us. If you say you're going to call us, call us. If you say you're going to show up at a certain time, show up. We need to be certain that you'll be there for us. Women want to know you're thinking about us when you're not with us. If you want to keep a woman happy, you need to let her know you're thinking about her when you can't be with her. We love romance. It doesn't matter whether we're eighteen or eighty years old. All women love romance.

This is where cell phones come in handy. A simple text message in the middle of the day works wonders to show a woman she's in your thoughts. Just don't use texting as your primary form of communication with her. If you do, you need to invest in my other book, **Facebook: The Greatest Passive Aggressive Weapon EVER**. Much of that book is devoted to the frustration with partners who prefer to communicate via texts and computers. Texts and internet postings make a great way to give her little confirmations during the day, but they can't be used as the sole form of communicating. Women need to hear your voice and engage in spontaneous conversations with you.

That doesn't mean women want needy men, either. They want to feel secure with you, but if you're too clingy, it will turn them off.

Patty and Jeff are living together now, and they attribute their union to Jeff's ability to give enough affection, but not *too* much. Jeff would call her to let her know he was thinking about her, but he didn't tell her everything about him. She knew enough to know he cared. While Jeff was busy with his own life, he carved out time to let Patty know she was on his mind.

Small gestures mean huge advances when you're trying to draw a woman closer to you. Thoughtful notes, texts, quick phone calls, and yes, Facebook posts go a long way with women. If she's your girlfriend, you better have her picture up on your personal web page. Some women may take this to an extreme degree.

Sheila counted all the pictures her boyfriend posted of her on his Facebook page, and then counted all the pictures he posted of other people. She was upset because the other people outnumbered her.

Okay, so we're not saying that some women don't get psycho. But we are saying that if you're dating us, we expect you to put our pictures up there with your other friends' photos. And don't hide us. Make reference to us if you're posting to friends about something you're doing with us. We want to know you're proud to be in a relationship with us. We want to feel secure in believing you're not trolling for other women online, making yourself available. If you're sitting next to us sending out tweets to say you're at the ballgame, we'll be upset if you don't say you're at the ballgame with *us*. Women have to feel safe and secure in relationships.

Take note of the little things. Women love it when you remember details and tidbits of information about them. Birthdays are obvious, but the not-so-obvious details win you brownie points. One man got his girlfriend a gift certificate to Merle Norman, because he noticed all her make-up came from that company. I was enamored with a man who came home from a business trip with a handful of cookbooks for me. While my three bookcases full of regional cookbooks are clearly hard to miss, he was the only man who ever thought to collect some for me when he was in a region I hadn't visited. Terryee felt more affectionate towards a man who asked her to tell him when she was PMSing, because he wanted to make sure he treated her extra special on those days, since they can be challenging for a woman's mood. And yes, he remembered the "special" days and showed up with chocolates and good humor.

Women are notorious for remembering the little details, as well as the big stuff. We won't forget your birthday, but we also remember you hate mushrooms. You won't find a mushroom anywhere near your slice of pizza, and we'd appreciate it if you'd remember we're deathly allergic to peanuts....before you put peanut butter in the Asian salad dressing we're about to eat. Saves on medical bills, as well as relationship hassles.

Women like you to show her you love her in five or six different ways. It's not that we don't like to hear you profess your love for us when we're making love, but we want you to say those words at other times, too. When you give us a compliment, don't be trying to kiss on us when you're talking. Verbally pay us a compliment when there's nothing in it for you.

Use the "sandwich method" when you want something from us. Sandwich your "want" in between two compliments. "You're beautiful," and "I love you," can sandwich the bologna you're slipping into the middle. We won't even shirk at the request to pick up your dry cleaning in the middle of the complimentary bread slices.

Listen to us. Nothing makes a woman feel more disregarded than when you don't listen to her. So in spite of the long day *you* just had, please listen to us when we are talking to you. You may be quizzed on it later.

Often men balk at the expectations that a woman is placing on them. You *know* if they're unreasonable or *normal* expectations. *Most* women are thoughtful and considerate when it comes to the man they love. Think back to all the little things she's done to make *your* life easier before you try to get out of showing up for her. In this case, my dad's advice may resonate more than ours does. Dad said, "I've learned that sometimes you just need to do things in order to keep the peace. So I do them, even if I don't want to. I just want to keep the peace.....my *own* fucking peace."

Online Dating

How do you entice the perfect partner with a two paragraph profile? For starters, you don't start off by displaying a picture of yourself that's ten years old and specify the most important quality you're looking for in a mate is Honesty. You have to *be* the partner you're looking for. If you're sending out a false advertisement, guess what the universe will send back to you?

So let's keep it real. Terryee and I have both successfully navigated the world of internet dating, and we've got some pointers to share. But first, my deceased son, Mikey, has some advice of his own.

When Mikey came through in a channeling session, I inquired about the book I was writing about him. I had written some funny stories about him, but I was wondering if I should try to put more of a serious spin on the whole book. Mikey came through a channeling session and told me, "Leave the funny parts in the book. The love is what resonates with them long after they've read the book. But the humor is what draws them in."

So take Mikey's advice and remember, "The humor is what draws them in." Humorous profiles always get more responses, especially from men. Men are inundated with women who are hot on the chase for their soul mate. No, make that, their husband.

Ladies, listen up. Men view a first meeting as just that: a first meeting to determine if there is some chemistry between you, but nothing more. They are not picking out china in their heads. They view it as an opportunity to see what you *really* look like, and they are also hoping you will have chemistry between your personalities. But they are not closing down all of their other matches, and will not do so until they are sure they want to forge a much closer relationship with you. You need to keep the same mindset. A first meeting is just a first get-to-know-ya introduction. If you like the guy, don't race home to close out your other matches, or cancel dates with other potential suitors. And *don't* feel upset when you notice he is still online and looking. Many of the dating sites allow you to see who is online, and some will show you the last time one of your matches logged on. Don't stalk their profile to see how many times they've been trolling after you met. Believe in the universal law of attraction! The right man will come to you if you're open to him. If the guy you just met is not the right one, you don't want him anyway! So don't try to force every guy you meet to be Mr. Right. Sometimes, all you really need is Mr. Right Now.

We view dating as a way to make new friends. If a friendship should turn into something more, then that's wonderful. But if not, we have still made a new friend. Some of the men we've met online have become some of our best friends. Some men have ended up becoming invaluable networking connections for career or personal matters. And yes, a few of them have become romantic loves. Just keep your mind open, as well as your heart. And don't buy the china just yet.

When you're trying to write a profile, ask yourself, "What do *I* want in a mate, and do I match up with that myself?" Like attracts like. You need to *be* the partner you want for yourself, before you demand the same.

Many people fall into the mindset of asking, "What does my *match* want in a partner?" This isn't about them. It's about you. What do *you* want? You need to be clear in your own mind about the qualities you desire in a partner.

If you love to read and it's important to you that your partner can carry on a conversation with you involving literary works, then you want to make that clear in your profile. If you get matched up with a man who says the last book he read was the March 1979 edition of Auto Mechanics, then he is not your perfect mate.....no matter how handsome he looks! Don't try to conform yourself to fit someone else's wish-list. It won't work in the long run.

We've read profiles of men who didn't interest us, and then noticed they changed their profiles to sound similar to our own when they contacted us. Really?? That red flag is as ominous as the red sky of the apocalypse. Run for cover.

While it's important to have a clear idea of the qualities your ideal mate should possess, it's not a good idea to put a laundry list on your profile. It's a major turn-off for both women and men when they're presented with a list of demands before they've even met the person. While we respect people who know what they want in a partner, we cringe at the profiles that fill up a page with lines that begin, "You are this. You are that. You must be this and that..." These people would be much better off saying, "I am this. I am that. I am looking for the same in a partner." It doesn't sound so egotistical and judgmental. Although, at least those people are being honest about one thing: they are control freaks. We are too evolved to waste time with someone who wants to tell us what to wear and how to behave around them.

Everyone has been hurt in love. Don't wear your bitterness on your sleeve, or in your screen name. Did the guy who called himself "DontLie2Me" really expect a response from a woman who is by nature, forgiving and happy? How about the woman who wanted a man with no emotional baggage from previous relationships? Was "TwiceBitten" the best screen name to show him the same applies to her?

If you've got an axe to grind with the opposite sex, get off the dating web site and get on with fixing yourself first. Your anger and bitterness will seep out and damage any potential new relationships. You will attract suitors who also have an axe with the same brand. You might as well put up a profile banner that reads, "Cheaters and Liars Welcome!" Anyone with the same issues will be attracted like a magnet. Keep in mind; they may be working on those issues from another angle. Rather than attracting someone else who has been hurt by betrayal, you may just attract another betrayer. In the end, you will both be working through the same issue surrounding trust. If you've had enough lessons in the trust school already, then make sure you're approaching any new relationship from a loving standpoint, or you will be setting yourself up for another semester of school. If you're putting out anger and bitterness, that's what you will get back.

What qualities do you love about yourself? Those are the qualities you should display in your profile. You want to attract someone who values those qualities as much as you do. It doesn't matter if you think it's an unusual or boring quality. It will be exciting to the right partner.

We can't reiterate enough the importance of being honest and real. If you are truly looking to meet a long-term partner, you're not helping yourself if you're trying to paint a different picture of yourself. Although, we give kudos to the gorgeous woman who posted the least flattering photo of herself available. She *was* being real. She wanted a man who valued her passion for gardening more than her beautiful face. And she found one. That guy should have bought a lottery ticket the day he finally saw her in person. Jackpot day!

Guys, please, take off the hats and shades. Do you want the lady to recognize you when you meet? Do you think women honestly believe you're hiding a full head of hair underneath that baseball cap? And if they do, are you planning on wearing the cap to bed if the relationship should progress to that? If you are seriously hoping to meet a potential mate, your photos should look like the person your mate will be meeting. Otherwise, you will usually disappoint them, and then you will end up being the one who is disappointed.

How long should you wait before you meet them? Here's where opinions often vary, but the most logical answer is *when you feel comfortable*. We are both big advocates of meeting right away, but not without a phone call first. Sometimes two people connect well in writing, but once you hear each other's voice over the phone, you already know there's no chemistry. It's easier to get off the phone with someone who doesn't interest you than it is to leave the coffee bar before your latte gets cold. (We don't like to be rude.)

Several of our friends have actually spent months writing back and forth with people they met online and were convinced they were falling in love. This has two pitfalls. The obvious one is that when they finally met, one of them did not feel any physical attraction for the other one. They had become so close in the months leading up to their first meeting; it was very difficult for one to essentially "breakup" on the first date. It was heartbreaking for the other one. The second problem with the lengthy online courtship is that it increases the amount of normal anxiety you feel on a first date. The first meeting has now become loaded with expectations and insecurities that you wouldn't normally have on a first date. Most of us don't make the best impression when we're full of anxiety.

So let's get back to your dating profile. You want to paint an honest picture of yourself without sounding depressing. You want to show them you're a loving, lovable human being, if they can live with ten sick old cats that pee on the carpet. You want to let them know you have a great sense of humor when you're not having one of your legendary crying jags. Most importantly, you'd like to convey your loyal, monogamous nature, as you chat with twenty other matches. You see what humor does?

Look at your life and ask, what have I done for the last seven or eight months? Dance? Workout? Travel? Read? If you haven't seen a ski slope in years, don't say you're "an avid skier." But if you honestly would like to go skiing in the immediate future, you can pique someone's interest by saying, "I have not been skiing for years, but I would love to find someone to join me in my heroic efforts to disembark from a moving gondola." The self-effacing humor and honesty will appeal to both expert and novice skiers alike. Same applies for "working out." The love of "working out" seems to be the most common lie on the dating web sites, and it's the easiest lie to detect upon first meeting. If your primary form of physical exercise is walking to the mailbox, don't put yourself out there as a gym rat. If you are *truly* beginning a new exercise program, then say something like, "I recently purchased a gym membership and would love to have a partner who will make sure I get my twenty-four ninety-five a month value out of it, with no renewal fees. And a free t-shirt." Once again, you're stating your honest intentions, but no one is expecting you to look like a fitness guru.

Have you always wanted to learn how to tango? Then say *that*. Don't broadcast yourself as a dancer. You'd be surprised at how many people will contact you, offering to take those ballroom dancing classes with you. Ditto for painting, pottery, and yoga. So if you have a secret longing to explore a new passion, that's not only a great icebreaker, but it's a great way to enliven a profile that might otherwise look dull. None of us are dull. But not all of us look exciting on paper. Men who are deep thinkers fascinate us. But if we were presented with a profile of a man who states he "loves to sit and think" in his free time, would we pursue that connection? Maybe not, but we would melt over the guy who says, "I love pondering the mysteries of life and contemplating what lies beyond this existence; when will time stop; and why did Mrs. Howell pack so many clothes for a three hour tour?"

When you're reading the profiles of your matches, take note of their degree of independence. If they state they are looking for a committed relationship and desire children, believe them. If they simply state they are looking to date, they are already telling you they're not desiring a major commitment. If *you* are, then leave that casual dater for others to pursue. They are not going to marry you.

Here's a question men need to ask themselves: Have you spent most of your life taking care of women? If you are accustomed to the traditional male role as the 'provider,' can you really handle a woman who is successful and independent? If you get satisfaction from taking care of a woman who depends on you, you won't feel the same control over your situation with a highly independent woman. She may look exciting, but would that relationship really feel comfortable to you? Remember, this is about *you*. What do *you* want in a partner?

Be honest about your habits. If you smoke, don't say you're a non-smoker. If you drink a bottle of wine every night, don't say you drink socially "on occasion."

> Paul met Linda on a dating site, and she professed to be a non-smoker. Paul is a radiologist, and health care is not only his business, but it's a way of life for him. He discovered Linda was a closet smoker after several dates, and Paul told her he just could not date anyone who smoked. Linda assured Paul she would quit, as she did not want to lose him over a cigarette. When Paul was convinced Linda had quit smoking, he surprised her with a vacation to Cancun. Two days into their

vacation, Paul discovered Linda was still sneaking cigarettes. He left her in Cancun and flew home that day. As Paul said, it was not just the smoking, but the even bigger issue here was lying.

What kind of visions do you have for yourself in the future, and does the other person's profile match that? If you have a few non-negotiable plans for your own future, keep that in mind when you're exchanging greetings. This can go beyond marriage and kids. Are you cemented in the town you live in, and does this person want to live somewhere else? Are you both in Kansas but *you* are planning on settling in Miami?

David admitted to having a hard time deciding if a particular woman was right for him. She had a great personality and similar interests. He asked her a question about retirement, and she said she couldn't wait to retire and be able to just sit and relax every day. David said he knew she wasn't the right partner for him then. He can't even imagine retiring and doing nothing, as there are still so many things he wants to do. He doesn't want a partner who doesn't have the same drive to keep achieving things.

So while you're throwing lines into the fish pond, you need to keep your own desires in the front of your mind. What do you want in a partner? And do you match up with that? If you want the total package, you have to *be* the total package....no matter what the package looks like. *You're* the one who wants to open it. *We* don't want to see what's inside. Eeew.

The Archangels

This is not an all-encompassing list, and there are many more angels that are not considered "archangels." But we chose the archangels that we regularly invoke in prayers for love and relationships. Sorry, we can't give you a specific angel for money. If one existed, he would be so overworked he might fall into the depression of victimhood himself, and we're pretty sure that doesn't exist in heaven.

Archangel Michael helps manifest abundance in career, love, anything you want. He is the lord of the angels in the Bible. In Hebrew, "Michael" means "who is as God." He is often depicted wearing armor and yielding his Sword of Truth. Archangel Michael protects us against negativity. Since manifesting requires the opposite of negative thinking, we call on Michael's strength for manifestation prayers. He stands for protection and power, and he's the guardian of truth.

Archangel Gabriel guides communication. Gabriel means "God is my strength," in Hebrew. Gabriel is often called "God's messenger angel." Archangel Gabriel is the bringer of truth and revelation. Call on Gabriel to help reveal information that will help you on your journey, and ask Gabriel for assistance in speaking your own truth

Archangel Raphael is the healing angel. In Hebrew, Raphael means, "God has healed." Raphael helps in all manners of healing; emotional, physical, and spiritual. Call on Archangel Raphael to assist you on a personal level, as well as assisting the world on a global healing level.

Archangel Chamuel's name has two interpretations. It comes from a Hebrew verb that means "comfort and compassion," but also is said to mean "He who sees God." Archangel Chamuel is the angel of love. He not only helps heal love in relationships, he guides us back down the path to loving ourselves, as well as experiencing the joy of unconditional love all around us. Archangel Chamuel can also help guide us in our journey to find our heart's desire in career and life purpose fulfillment. Chamuel can inspire us with thoughts of love to forgive and show compassion. Chamuel will help you when your heart is broken or you feel fearful, by bringing you his comforting presence of love.

Mantras, Meditations and Prayers

Repetition is the key to success in manifesting. Constant focus on your intentions can be achieved by giving yourself continual mental reminders of those intentions throughout the day. It's easy to develop a lackadaisical attitude when real life keeps you busy. But while it may seem difficult to find any spare time to devote to focusing on your manifesting meditations, keep in mind that you will not achieve that life you desire without focused intentions. When your boss, your spouse, your client, your child, your business is demanding every minute of your time, don't allow yourself to neglect your own desires because you are so wrapped up in meeting the demands that everyone else is placing on your time. You can mentally recite a short mantra in your head in between your heroic acts of putting out fires for others. In fact, you can mentally focus on a mantra when you are standing in an elevator, or pumping gas, or taking a pee. You don't need to block out long hours of your day for meditation, although we would all be much happier if we could! You can focus on your mantra while you're doing anything that doesn't require speaking to another person or concentrating on something that might bring harm to you or another without your full attention: Walking on the treadmill, polishing your nails, weeding the garden, pretending to read the newspaper, cooking or cleaning, etc. As long as you have a free moment to "think" your mantra to yourself, you will take a step towards manifesting that desire every time you focus your intent upon it.

We are giving you some sample meditations to use, but you can create your own unique mantra for manifesting your own personal desires for abundance. Depending on your personal beliefs, you may choose to invoke a higher power, or you may just put your intentions out to the universe. Since we frequently get asked about our belief in angels and their domains, we are including them in these meditations. But remember, your mantra will not be effective for you unless you believe in the words you are saying. Every word counts. Every word must 'feel' right to you. If there is one word that carries a negative feeling for you, then you're wasting your time with your mantra. You're basically standing there wearing a red shirt while telling the universe you're wearing a blue shirt. If it feels wrong, you don't believe it yourself. And the whole concept here is *believing* it yourself. Every single word must carry a positive believable vibration for you.

Here's a mantra called, "The I am's." Yes, that's a very technical name, of course, because every sentence begins with the words, "I am." Did you think we were rocket scientists? The "I am" mantra is one of the easiest meditations. You can pick two or three things that you want to manifest for, and easily memorize your mantra. That way, you can repeat it anytime throughout the day, up in your head or aloud.

I am balanced and happy on all levels; mind, body, and spirit.

I am an amazing soul and spiritual being.

I am showing up for myself and my partner.

I'm experiencing total happiness and love with him/her.

I am taking care of the inner child inside of me to make sure I feel safe and secure.

I am connecting to the source energy within me.

I am giving and receiving unconditional love with my partner.

I am healing the competitive nature within me. I am the best in every area of my life and I know that I am connected to all that is.

I am abundant in every area of my life.

I am worthy.

You can tailor your own "I Am's" to fit whatever you're manifesting. You don't need to have a mate to say, "I am showing up for my partner." In fact, that's part of the whole idea. You're calling your soul mate into you by opening yourself up to that feeling of being completely supportive and loving towards them.

If you're hoping to buy a new house, then say something like, "I am moving to the home of my dreams," or "I am enjoying the freedom of owning my own home." Remember that *feeling* comes before *thinking*. Feel the love or contentment that you know you'll derive out of whatever it is you're manifesting, while you're saying the words.

Prayer for Abundance

Dear Archangel Michael,

Thank you for helping me manifest abundance and opportunities in my life. Thank you for your guidance and help in discovering and developing my life purpose. I trust and have faith with you by my side, guiding me on this journey.

Prayer for Uniting with Soul Mate, Companion or Twin Flame

Thank you Jesus and Archangel Chamuel, for uniting myself and my mate on a soul level with this prayer. Thank you for preparing us both to meet in divine and perfect timing. If there is anything I need to be aware of, in order to make this union the most holy of unions, please show me with thoughts, dreams, and feelings. I honor my soul mate and myself with this holy union. Thank you very much.

Prayer for Physical and Emotional Healing

Thank you Jesus and Archangel Raphael. I give thanks for perfect alignment of mind, body, and spirit. Heal my heart and mind and body, so that I will come from a place of desire in whatever I choose.

Healing Specific Areas from Raphael

Archangel Raphael can be invoked to heal specific physical and emotional problems. Use a white and/or a blue candle and do the breathing exercise. Think about the injured part of your body as healthy and whole; not as sick and needing healing. This is the same for the emotional challenges. Think of yourself as happy and healed.

Thank you, Raphael, for healing this part of me. (Describe the situation.) *Please allow the reason I chose this situation to be revealed to me in dreams, thoughts, or in meditation.*

There is a reason why you chose this situation on a soul level, and ask to know the reason why. When you understand the reason, you will heal this on a deeper level.

Prayer for Removing Blocks

This is directed to Jesus, the ascended master, and Archangel for the blocks we come into this life to heal.

Dear Jesus and Archangel Michael, thank you for helping me heal this situation. (Describe the situation and the block that you have identified within yourself, or with the person you have a conflict with.) *Show me how to come from a place of nonjudgmental love.*

Terryee uses a white candle with this prayer. Light the candle and take a few deep breaths. Think about how your body is feeling as you're breathing. Center yourself with the breathing exercise before reciting the prayer.

Maintaining Clear Communication with God

Dear Holy Father and God Almighty, Thank you for bringing me, your holy child, the highest and best good for myself. I appreciate the choices you have given to create the best life possible to share.

Prayer for Abundance

Okay, so I didn't give full disclosure on the "money angel" thing, but I didn't actually lie. Lakshmi and Ganesha are not considered "angels." Lakshmi is an ascended master; a Hindu goddess of prosperity (in both spiritual and material), wealth, and fortune. She protects her devotees against troubles related to money, as well as other misery. She is considered the "goddess of wealth" by her worshippers. Terryee works with Lakshmi in bringing both happiness and prosperity. It's important to do the breathing exercises first, as it centers you so that you can connect with your heart and your higher power.

Thank you, Lakshmi, for bringing happiness and love in my heart, and prosperity and abundance in my physical life. (Describe the situation. For example; money, job, house, apartment.)

Removing Blocks with Ganesha (Ganesh)

Ganesh is a Hindu deity that is widely recognized because he's depicted with an elephant head. He is revered as the Lord of Beginnings, Remover of Obstacles, and Lord of Obstacles. Ganesh is wonderful for bringing prosperity and removing obstacles so that prosperity comes to you. Terryee recommends working with Lakshmi and Ganesh in tandem. She uses green or pink candles because they represent heart energy. Light the candles and do your breathing exercise.

Thank you, Ganesh, for bringing prosperity and removing the obstacles that may be blocking me. This includes spiritual, emotional, and physical blocks. I choose to come from the highest and best good for myself and others.

Finding Your Life Purpose

Dear Michael and Chamuel, I would like to know my life purpose. Thank you for giving me thoughts and ideas to show me what my purpose is. (If you have an idea what it may be, describe it and ask for guidance and confirmation.)

Do the breathing exercise. While you are focused on your breathing, think back to when you were a child and what you dreamed of doing. This is a place to start, and then say the prayer. Purple and white candles are good to use in this situation.

*Angels and guides are thought to be drawn to candlelight because the natural burning energy illuminates and purifies the air.

Prayer to Aengus, Ascended Master, for Twin Flame/Twin Soul Relationships

Terryee wanted to share some information about Aengus, after he connected with her during a meditation:

> *Aengus is beautiful, calm, and he has a gentle feel to him. I saw him with beautiful blond hair and a harp. I asked him these three questions: How can we connect with him? How do we work with him on a daily basis? And how can he help you find romance that will lead to a potential mate, if you choose?*

> *This is his response to my first question about how to connect with him. We connect to him by playing soft music, especially music with a harp. Light three candles: a blue one for the communication (throat) chakra; a purple one for the intuition chakra (third eye); and a white candle for the crown chakra. This connects you to all that is.*

> *Then sit quietly and think about the music and breathing in and out for a few minutes. Aengus gave me prayer you can say to him.*

Dear Aengus, thank you for coming to guide me in my relationship. I would like your help (State your request). I appreciate you working with me.

Here is his response to my second question: How does someone work with you on a daily basis? He told me the most important thing to remember when working with him is your intention. Keep it clear. Do not waver. If you are dating the person who is your mate or you are looking for a future mate. It is important to feel complete yourself, without looking for someone to complete you. When we realize we are already whole and complete, then we'll meet someone to date or marry. It is about sharing yourself with that person, but not about that person completing you. You are already everything. You have found it in yourself first and then you will attract that complete person in someone else.

In response to my third question, Aengus said he can help you more if you make a list of all the qualities you would like to experience in a mate. Start with the ones you like about yourself first. Make sure you include the spiritual, emotional and physical qualities you are looking for. Read these qualities before you go to bed and before you leave in the morning. You will become clear on the qualities you are looking for, and they will become a part of your conscious and unconscious self, if you say them every day. I asked him why this is so important. He told me when you know what you are looking for in your mate, I can help bring this person to you. The qualities that you describe for your potential mate or existing one are important. When you read those qualities aloud every day, your vibration increases and your self-worth elevates. You see the qualities that are important to you in yourself first. Reciting the qualities once or twice a day keeps your intention focused. Your intention is a force. It is strong and powerful. You always want your intentions to work for you and help you create a life of prosperity. Speaking these qualities and engaging in prayer or meditation every day will attract the soul mate or twin flame you desire to experience a great relationship with. – Terryee

The ceremony of lighting candles, praying, or reciting mantras makes us feel like we're at least "doing something" to help ourselves, and that's always a step in the right direction mentally. When you feel like you have some tools to help yourself, you instantly feel a little more optimistic, a tad more positive. That's the feeling we're trying to instill in you. But don't get too carried away with the candles. I was horrified when I awoke one morning to discover I had left a candle burning all night. Nothing was harmed, but I realized it could have been a disaster. I didn't tell anyone else about my absent-minded mishap, but *somebody* knew. Terryee called to inform me that my son had come through to her, and asked her to tell me to be careful with the candles. Mikey said, "I can do a lot of things but I can't drag her out of a burning building."

We hope this book has given you some ideas to start making your own dreams come true. Terryee and I have both experienced success using these principles, and we've seen countless others realize their own dreams through manifesting and mantras. Yeah, we know, you're saying you'll feel stupid reciting, "I am a beautiful woman," when you're actually a man. We agree. Everything in this book is meant to be tailored to fit your specific dreams, your life, and the kind of love *you* want. Most importantly, it's meant to fit you; the *real* you. We want you to find your authentic self: The one that's buried beneath all the rubbish of your ego's making; the 'you' that keeps getting kicked around by your own fear.

We're not promising you'll instantly feel like a fairy princess riding on a white fluffy cloud of higher consciousness, but even Terryee says, "I may hear angels, but I'm not ridin' those damn unicorns."

Shoot us an email if you liked the book, hated the book, or just feel snobbish indifference towards the book. We'd love to hear your comments. Just don't ask Terryee if you're going to win the lottery. You didn't buy a ticket, dumbass.

Diane@DianeBucci.com

Terryee@AngelCoaches.org

www.ingramcontent.com/pod-product-compliance
Lightning Source LLC
LaVergne TN
LVHW021509080426
835509LV00018B/2459